Fabrice Houdart

Fighting for LGBTQ Rights at the UN – Unauthorized

Amani Malik

ISBN: 9781779696021
Imprint: Telephasic Workshop

Contents

A Belgian Childhood

Fabrice Houdart's journey towards becoming a renowned LGBTQ activist began in the heart of Europe, specifically in the vibrant city of Brussels, Belgium. Born into a family that valued education and culture, Fabrice's early years were painted with the rich hues of Belgian heritage, from the delectable chocolates to the enchanting architecture that adorned the streets. However, beneath this picturesque facade lay a world of complexities that would shape his identity and ignite his passion for activism.

Growing up in Brussels, a city known for its multiculturalism, Fabrice was exposed to a diverse array of perspectives and lifestyles. This melting pot of cultures played a pivotal role in his formative years, as he navigated the intricacies of his own identity. The juxtaposition of traditional Belgian values and the burgeoning acceptance of LGBTQ rights created a backdrop that was both comforting and challenging.

$$\text{Identity Formation} = f(\text{Cultural Exposure}, \text{Family Values}, \text{Social Environment}) \tag{1}$$

This equation illustrates that Fabrice's identity formation was a function of various factors, including cultural exposure from his surroundings, the values instilled by his family, and the social environment he was immersed in. Each component contributed to his understanding of self and the world around him.

As he transitioned from childhood to adolescence, Fabrice began to grapple with his sexuality. The internal conflict was palpable; he experienced moments of joy and acceptance interspersed with fear and confusion. The struggle for self-acceptance was compounded by societal expectations and the lingering stigma surrounding LGBTQ identities. It was during these turbulent years that Fabrice discovered his passion for activism.

$$\text{Activism} = \text{Awareness} \times \text{Empathy} \tag{2}$$

This equation signifies that Fabrice's activism was fueled by a heightened awareness of the injustices faced by the LGBTQ community, coupled with a profound sense of empathy for those who suffered. His early encounters with discrimination, both personally and observed in others, ignited a fire within him—a desire to advocate for change.

Fabrice found solace and support among friends and mentors who embraced his identity. These relationships became a cornerstone of his journey, providing him with the encouragement needed to embrace his true self. It was through these connections that he learned the importance of community and solidarity in the face of adversity.

In high school, Fabrice took his first steps into activism, standing up for LGBTQ rights among his peers. He organized events that celebrated diversity and fostered dialogue, creating a safe space for students to express themselves without fear of judgment. His determination was unwavering, as he understood the significance of representation and visibility in a society that often marginalized queer voices.

$$\text{Visibility} = \text{Representation} + \text{Advocacy} \tag{3}$$

This equation encapsulates Fabrice's belief that visibility in the LGBTQ community is achieved through representation and advocacy. By amplifying voices that were often silenced, he aimed to challenge the status quo and inspire others to join the fight for equality.

As Fabrice navigated the complexities of adolescence, he emerged not only as a young man coming to terms with his identity but also as a budding activist ready to challenge societal norms. His experiences in Belgium laid the groundwork for a lifelong commitment to fighting for LGBTQ rights, setting the stage for the impactful work he would later undertake on a global scale.

In summary, Fabrice Houdart's Belgian childhood was a tapestry woven with threads of culture, identity, struggle, and resilience. It was in this environment that he first learned the power of advocacy and the importance of standing up for oneself and others. These early experiences would prove to be the catalyst for his future endeavors, as he embarked on a journey that would take him from the streets of Brussels to the halls of the United Nations, championing the rights of LGBTQ individuals worldwide.

A Belgian Childhood

Fabrice Houdart was born into a world that was as rich in culture as it was in complexity, nestled in the heart of Brussels, Belgium. Growing up in this vibrant city, known for its historic architecture and delicious waffles, Fabrice's early years were marked by a tapestry of experiences that would shape his identity and fuel his passion for activism.

Brussels, the de facto capital of the European Union, was not only a melting pot of languages and traditions but also a place where Fabrice would confront the realities of being different. His childhood was a whirlwind of emotions, filled with laughter, discovery, and the occasional pang of loneliness. As he navigated the cobblestone streets of his neighborhood, Fabrice began to understand that his journey would not be a straight path, but rather a winding road filled with twists and turns.

1.1.1 Growing up in Brussels, Belgium

In the heart of Brussels, Fabrice's early life was painted with the colors of diversity. Surrounded by a mosaic of cultures, he learned to appreciate the beauty of differences from a young age. His parents, both educators, instilled in him a love for learning and an understanding of the importance of empathy. They often took him to local festivals, exposing him to various customs and traditions, which sparked his curiosity about the world around him.

However, as Fabrice grew older, he began to feel the weight of societal expectations. In a society that often struggled with acceptance, he grappled with feelings of isolation, particularly as he started to recognize his own sexuality. The vibrant streets of Brussels, which once felt like a playground, began to feel like a maze filled with obstacles. This internal conflict would later become a catalyst for his activism.

1.1.2 Discovering his passion for activism

The turning point in Fabrice's childhood came during a school project on human rights. As he delved into the history of marginalized communities, he felt a spark igniting within him. The stories of those who fought against oppression resonated deeply with his own experiences of feeling different. It was during this time that Fabrice discovered the power of advocacy and the importance of standing up for what is right.

Inspired by figures like Martin Luther King Jr. and Nelson Mandela, Fabrice began to understand that activism was not just about shouting for justice; it was about creating a dialogue and fostering understanding. He organized small gatherings at school to discuss LGBTQ issues, inviting classmates to share their thoughts and experiences. These discussions, though met with mixed reactions, laid the groundwork for his future endeavors.

1.1.3 Coming to Terms

As Fabrice navigated the complexities of adolescence, he found himself at a crossroads. The struggle with his sexuality was a constant battle, often leaving him feeling like a ship lost at sea. He grappled with self-acceptance, questioning whether he could be true to himself in a world that sometimes felt hostile. Yet, amidst the turmoil, he found solace in the support of friends and mentors who encouraged him to embrace his identity.

Fabrice's friends became his lifeline, offering a safe space where he could express his fears and dreams without judgment. They celebrated his victories and provided comfort during his defeats, reminding him that he was not alone in his journey. It was through these connections that Fabrice began to recognize the importance of community and the strength that comes from shared experiences.

1.1.4 High School Activism

Armed with newfound confidence and a desire to make a difference, Fabrice took his first steps into the world of activism during high school. He organized events that aimed to raise awareness about LGBTQ rights, inviting speakers from local organizations to share their stories. These events not only educated his peers but also fostered a sense of solidarity among students who felt marginalized.

Fabrice's efforts did not go unnoticed. He faced resistance from some school administrators who were wary of discussing LGBTQ issues openly. However, undeterred, he continued to push for change, believing that dialogue was essential for progress. His determination and resilience became a beacon of hope for many, inspiring others to join the fight for equality.

1.1.5 Conclusion

Fabrice Houdart's Belgian childhood was a crucible of experiences that forged his identity and ignited his passion for activism. From the vibrant streets of Brussels to the struggles of self-acceptance, each moment played a crucial role in shaping the advocate he would become. As he embarked on his journey toward fighting for LGBTQ rights, the lessons learned during these formative years would serve as a foundation for a lifetime dedicated to creating a more inclusive world.

ERROR. thisXsection() returned an empty string with textbook depth = 3.

ERROR. thisXsection() returned an empty string with textbook depth = 3.

ERROR. thisXsection() returned an empty string with textbook depth = 3.

Discovering his passion for activism

As Fabrice Houdart navigated the vibrant streets of Brussels, he began to uncover a profound passion for activism that would shape his life and the lives of countless others. This journey of self-discovery was not merely a personal endeavor; it was a response to the societal challenges he witnessed around him. The seeds of his activism were planted during his formative years, and they began to sprout as he became increasingly aware of the injustices faced by the LGBTQ community.

In Belgium, a country known for its progressive stance on many social issues, Fabrice found himself in a paradox. While same-sex marriage was legalized in 2003, discrimination and prejudice still lingered in the shadows. This dissonance ignited a fire within him. He realized that laws alone could not eradicate the deep-seated biases that permeated society. Thus, he embarked on a quest to understand the dynamics of social change and the role of activism in fostering equality.

Fabrice's first foray into activism was inspired by the stories of those around him—friends who faced discrimination, family members who struggled with acceptance, and mentors who had dedicated their lives to the fight for LGBTQ rights. He began to read extensively about social justice movements, studying the theories of renowned activists like Harvey Milk and Marsha P. Johnson. The principles of intersectionality, as articulated by Kimberlé Crenshaw, resonated deeply with him, highlighting the importance of recognizing how various forms of oppression intersect.

This intellectual awakening was complemented by real-world experiences. Fabrice attended local LGBTQ events, where he met individuals who shared their experiences of marginalization and resilience. These encounters solidified his commitment to activism. One particularly impactful event was a candlelight vigil for victims of anti-LGBTQ violence, where Fabrice witnessed the power of community solidarity. The collective grief transformed into a rallying cry for justice, and he felt an overwhelming sense of responsibility to contribute to this cause.

As he delved deeper into the world of activism, Fabrice encountered several challenges. The LGBTQ community was not monolithic; it was a tapestry of diverse identities, each with its own unique struggles. Navigating these complexities required sensitivity and a willingness to listen. Fabrice learned the importance of allyship and the need to amplify marginalized voices within the movement. He began to understand that effective activism is not only about speaking out but also about creating spaces for others to share their stories.

In high school, Fabrice took the initiative to start an LGBTQ club, a safe haven for students to express themselves and find support. This endeavor was met with resistance from some school administrators, who questioned the necessity of such a group. However, Fabrice's unwavering determination shone through. He organized events that educated the student body about LGBTQ issues, fostering a culture of acceptance and understanding. The club became a beacon of hope, empowering students to embrace their identities and advocate for their rights.

Through these experiences, Fabrice discovered that activism was not merely a passion; it was a calling. He recognized that the fight for LGBTQ rights was intertwined with broader social justice movements, including those addressing racial inequality, gender discrimination, and economic injustice. This intersectional approach informed his activism, allowing him to build coalitions with other marginalized groups. He understood that true change could only be achieved through solidarity and collaboration.

In summary, Fabrice Houdart's journey of discovering his passion for activism was marked by a blend of personal experiences, intellectual exploration, and community engagement. He emerged as a determined advocate, ready to confront the challenges ahead. His story serves as a reminder that activism is not just about fighting for one's rights; it is about standing up for the rights of all individuals, fostering a world where everyone can live authentically and without fear.

Coming to Terms

Struggles with sexuality and self-acceptance

Fabrice Houdart's journey toward self-acceptance was not a straight path; it was more of a winding road filled with sharp turns, bumps, and the occasional pothole that threatened to derail his progress. Growing up in Brussels, Belgium, a city known for its rich history and cultural diversity, Fabrice faced the daunting task of reconciling his burgeoning identity with societal expectations. The struggle with sexuality is often intertwined with a myriad of psychological theories and personal experiences that shape one's self-acceptance.

One of the most prominent theories that can be applied to Fabrice's experience is the *Identity Development Theory* proposed by Erik Erikson. Erikson's stages of psychosocial development outline how individuals navigate various challenges throughout their lives. In the context of sexuality, the stage of *identity vs. role confusion* is particularly relevant, as it emphasizes the importance of forming a coherent sense of self during adolescence. Fabrice found himself grappling with questions of identity, often feeling torn between who he was and who society expected him to be.

The pressure to conform to heteronormative standards was palpable. Fabrice recalls moments in high school where he felt the weight of societal expectations pressing down on him, stifling his true self. The fear of rejection and ridicule loomed large, creating an internal conflict that manifested as anxiety and self-doubt. This struggle is not uncommon; many LGBTQ individuals experience what is known as *internalized homophobia*, a phenomenon where societal stigma leads individuals to harbor negative feelings about their own sexual orientation.

Fabrice's experience was compounded by the cultural backdrop of Belgium, where traditional values often clashed with the burgeoning acceptance of LGBTQ identities. He witnessed both acceptance and discrimination, leaving him in a state of confusion. In his early teenage years, Fabrice often found solace in the support of a close-knit group of friends who provided a safe space for him to explore his identity. These friendships became a lifeline, allowing him to express himself without fear of judgment. However, even within this supportive environment, the specter of self-doubt lingered.

$$S = \frac{C}{D} \tag{4}$$

In this equation, S represents self-acceptance, C symbolizes the level of support from friends and mentors, and D denotes the degree of societal discrimination faced. As Fabrice navigated his teenage years, the balance between these variables fluctuated. On days when his support system was strong, his self-acceptance soared; conversely, moments of societal rejection sent him spiraling into despair.

The turning point for Fabrice came during a pivotal moment in his high school experience. He decided to participate in an LGBTQ awareness event organized by a group of brave peers. The event was a celebration of diversity, featuring speakers who shared their own stories of struggle and triumph. For the first time, Fabrice felt a sense of belonging. The stories resonated with him, igniting a spark of hope that perhaps he, too, could embrace his identity without fear. This experience served as a catalyst for change, prompting him to confront his fears head-on.

Despite the progress he made, the journey toward self-acceptance was fraught with setbacks. There were days when Fabrice felt overwhelmed by the weight of societal expectations, leading him to retreat into a shell of self-doubt. He often found himself questioning whether he would ever fully accept himself. The internal dialogue was relentless, echoing the sentiments of many LGBTQ individuals who struggle with self-acceptance.

$$R = \sum_{i=1}^{n} (P_i - E_i)^2 \tag{5}$$

In this equation, R represents the level of resilience Fabrice developed over time, while P_i denotes the personal experiences he encountered, and E_i signifies the expectations imposed by society. As he began to accumulate positive experiences—such as supportive friendships, affirming mentors, and moments of self-discovery—his resilience grew, enabling him to challenge the negative narratives that had long plagued him.

Ultimately, Fabrice's journey toward self-acceptance was characterized by a gradual unfolding of identity. He learned that self-acceptance is not a destination but rather an ongoing process that requires patience, understanding, and compassion. It was through this realization that he began to embrace his true self, recognizing that his worth was not contingent upon societal validation.

In conclusion, the struggles with sexuality and self-acceptance that Fabrice Houdart faced during his formative years were a testament to the resilience of the human spirit. His experiences reflect a broader narrative shared by many in the LGBTQ community, highlighting the importance of support systems, personal growth, and the ongoing journey toward embracing one's true identity. As he moved forward in life, these early challenges would lay the groundwork for his future activism, fueling his passion for advocating for LGBTQ rights on a global scale.

Finding support and guidance in friends and mentors

Navigating the tumultuous waters of self-acceptance can feel like trying to balance on a tightrope strung between two skyscrapers. For Fabrice Houdart, this journey was made significantly easier by the presence of friends and mentors who provided invaluable support and guidance. The importance of a supportive network cannot be overstated, especially in the context of LGBTQ youth, where studies have shown that individuals with strong support systems are more likely to experience positive mental health outcomes.

The Role of Friends

Fabrice's friends were his lifeline during his formative years in Brussels. They were the ones who held his hand through the storm of confusion and fear that often accompanies the coming-out process. According to the *National LGBTQ Task Force*, friends can serve as a crucial buffer against the negative effects of societal stigma. They can provide a safe space for individuals to express their true selves without fear of judgment.

For instance, one of Fabrice's closest friends, Julie, was a beacon of light during his darkest moments. She encouraged him to embrace his identity, often reminding him of his worth and potential. Their late-night conversations, filled with laughter and tears, became a sanctuary where Fabrice could explore his feelings freely. This camaraderie exemplifies the *Social Support Theory*, which posits that emotional and informational support can significantly enhance an individual's coping mechanisms.

Mentorship Matters

While friends provided emotional support, mentors offered guidance and direction. Fabrice was fortunate to encounter several mentors who played pivotal roles in shaping his activism. One such mentor was Professor Alain Moreau, a renowned advocate for human rights at his university. Professor Moreau not only recognized Fabrice's potential but also actively encouraged him to pursue a career in advocacy.

Mentorship is critical in the LGBTQ community, where role models can often be scarce. According to *The Williams Institute*, having a mentor can lead to greater self-efficacy and increased likelihood of pursuing leadership roles. Fabrice's relationship with Professor Moreau is a prime example of how mentorship can provide the necessary tools to navigate the complexities of activism.

$$M = f(S, E, R) \tag{6}$$

Where M represents the effectiveness of mentorship, S is the support provided, E denotes the encouragement offered, and R signifies the resources made available to the mentee. This equation illustrates that the interplay of these factors can significantly enhance the mentee's journey toward self-acceptance and activism.

Building a Support Network

Fabrice's experience underscores the importance of actively building a support network. He learned that seeking out allies, whether through LGBTQ organizations or community groups, could provide both emotional and practical assistance. For example, joining the local LGBTQ youth group not only connected him with peers facing similar challenges but also exposed him to workshops and resources that empowered him to become a more effective advocate.

Research indicates that participation in such groups can lead to increased resilience and a sense of belonging, which are crucial for personal development. Fabrice's involvement in these organizations also provided him with opportunities to mentor others, creating a cycle of support that is vital for community growth.

Conclusion

In conclusion, finding support and guidance from friends and mentors was instrumental in Fabrice Houdart's journey toward self-acceptance and activism. The emotional backing from friends, combined with the strategic guidance from mentors, equipped him with the tools necessary to navigate the complexities of LGBTQ advocacy. As he continued to grow and evolve, Fabrice understood that the support he received was not just a lifeline but a foundation upon which he could build a legacy of change. This network of allies would not only bolster his confidence but also inspire him to become a beacon of hope for others in the LGBTQ community, demonstrating that no one has to walk this path alone.

High School Activism

Standing up for LGBTQ rights in school

Fabrice Houdart's high school years were not just a time of personal growth; they were a crucible for activism that would shape his future endeavors. In an environment that often mirrored the complexities of societal attitudes toward LGBTQ individuals, Fabrice found himself at the intersection of adolescence and advocacy.

During this period, he encountered a myriad of challenges that highlighted the pressing need for LGBTQ rights within educational institutions. The school environment, typically seen as a sanctuary for learning and development, often became a battleground for discrimination and prejudice. The theory of *social identity,* as posited by Henri Tajfel, suggests that individuals derive a sense of self from their group memberships, which can lead to in-group favoritism and out-group discrimination. This theory was palpably evident in Fabrice's school, where LGBTQ students frequently faced bullying and ostracization.

Fabrice recognized that standing up for LGBTQ rights in school was not merely about defending his identity; it was about creating a safe and inclusive environment for all students. He initiated discussions on the importance of respect and equality, often referencing the *Universal Declaration of Human Rights,* which asserts that "all human beings are born free and equal in dignity and rights." This foundational document served as a guiding principle for his advocacy, reinforcing the idea that LGBTQ rights are human rights.

One notable example of his activism occurred during a school assembly when a fellow student made derogatory remarks about LGBTQ individuals. Fabrice seized the moment to address the audience, employing rhetorical strategies that Jim Carrey might use—infusing humor and charisma to engage his peers while delivering a poignant message. He stated, "If we can laugh at our differences, why can't we celebrate them?" This comment not only lightened the mood but also prompted a wave of applause, illustrating the power of humor in activism.

Fabrice also organized events such as the first-ever LGBTQ Awareness Day at his school. He collaborated with teachers and administrators to create a safe space for discussions about sexual orientation and gender identity. The event featured guest speakers from local LGBTQ organizations, who shared their experiences and insights, thus fostering empathy and understanding among students. The success of this initiative was evident, as it led to the formation of a student-led LGBTQ club, which provided ongoing support and resources for students grappling with their identities.

Despite these achievements, Fabrice faced significant opposition. Some faculty members were resistant to discussions about LGBTQ issues, citing concerns about "promoting an agenda." This resistance highlighted the ongoing challenges within educational settings regarding LGBTQ advocacy. Fabrice countered this by emphasizing the importance of education in combating ignorance and prejudice. He often quoted the late Harvey Milk, who famously said, "You gotta give them hope." This became a mantra for Fabrice, reminding him that every conversation, every event, and every act of courage contributed to a larger movement for equality.

In conclusion, Fabrice's high school activism was marked by a blend of passion, humor, and resilience. His experiences laid the groundwork for his future work in LGBTQ advocacy, demonstrating that even in the face of adversity, standing up for what is right can inspire change. As he navigated the complexities of adolescence, he also forged a path for future generations, proving that schools can be incubators for social justice and equality. The lessons learned during this formative time would echo throughout his career, reinforcing the belief that activism begins at the grassroots level, often in the most unexpected places.

$$\text{Advocacy Impact} = \text{Awareness} \times \text{Engagement} \times \text{Action} \tag{7}$$

Organizing events and advocating for change

As Fabrice navigated the tumultuous waters of high school, he quickly realized that the best way to channel his passion for LGBTQ rights was through organizing events that would not only raise awareness but also foster a sense of community and solidarity among students. This period marked a pivotal moment in his journey as an activist, where he learned the intricacies of advocacy, the importance of visibility, and the power of collective action.

Understanding the Need for Advocacy

Fabrice's early experiences revealed a stark reality: many of his peers were unaware of the struggles faced by LGBTQ individuals. The lack of understanding often led to discrimination, bullying, and isolation. To combat this, he recognized that education was paramount. He began by organizing workshops and informational sessions at his school, inviting speakers from local LGBTQ organizations to share their stories and educate students about the importance of acceptance and equality.

Event Organization: The Blueprint for Change

To effectively organize events, Fabrice employed a structured approach that included the following steps:

1. **Identifying Objectives:** Fabrice understood that each event needed a clear purpose. Whether it was to celebrate Pride Month, commemorate the Transgender Day of Remembrance, or simply create a safe space for dialogue, setting clear objectives helped guide the planning process.

2. **Building a Team:** Realizing that he couldn't do it alone, Fabrice recruited like-minded peers who shared his passion. Together, they formed an LGBTQ club that became a hub for advocacy and activism within the school community.

3. **Securing Resources:** Fabrice learned the importance of resource management. This included securing funding, whether through school budgets or local sponsorships, and finding venues that could accommodate their events.

4. **Marketing and Outreach:** To ensure maximum participation, Fabrice utilized social media platforms, school newsletters, and posters to spread the word. He crafted messages that resonated with students, emphasizing inclusivity and the importance of standing together against discrimination.

5. **Evaluating Impact:** After each event, Fabrice and his team conducted surveys to gather feedback. This helped them understand what worked, what didn't, and how they could improve future initiatives.

Examples of Events and Their Impact

Among the many events Fabrice organized, one of the most impactful was the "Unity in Diversity" fair. This event brought together various cultural and social groups within the school to celebrate diversity. It featured booths, performances, and discussions that highlighted the intersectionality of LGBTQ identities with other social movements.

The fair not only fostered a sense of belonging among LGBTQ students but also educated their heterosexual peers. Fabrice noted that conversations sparked during this event led to lasting friendships and alliances, breaking down barriers of misunderstanding and prejudice.

Another notable event was the "Speak Out" forum, where students were invited to share their experiences with bullying and discrimination. This platform allowed for vulnerable storytelling, creating a safe environment for healing and support. Fabrice's role as a moderator was crucial; he facilitated discussions that encouraged empathy and active listening, promoting a culture of respect within the school.

Challenges and Resilience

Despite his successes, Fabrice faced significant challenges. Organizing events often met resistance from school administration, particularly when discussing sensitive topics. He encountered pushback from peers who did not understand the need for LGBTQ advocacy. However, these obstacles only fueled his determination.

Fabrice learned to navigate these challenges by employing strategic advocacy. He gathered data on the prevalence of bullying and discrimination in his school, presenting it to the administration to illustrate the need for change. His resilience in the face of adversity became a hallmark of his activism, inspiring others to stand up for what they believed in.

Conclusion: The Ripple Effect of Advocacy

Through organizing events and advocating for change, Fabrice not only amplified LGBTQ voices within his school but also laid the groundwork for future activism. His experiences taught him that advocacy is not just about raising awareness; it's about creating a movement that empowers individuals to embrace their identities and stand together against injustice. This foundational work would later serve as a springboard for his endeavors on a global scale, illustrating the profound impact that grassroots activism can have on the larger fight for LGBTQ rights.

College Bound

Choosing to study Law and International Relations

As Fabrice Houdart approached the end of his high school years, he found himself at a crossroads, a moment of decision that would shape not only his career but also his life's mission. The vibrant city of Brussels, with its rich tapestry of cultures and political institutions, provided the perfect backdrop for his burgeoning interests in law and international relations. It was here that Fabrice's passion for activism began to crystallize, fueled by a desire to create a more just and equitable world for the LGBTQ community.

The Call of Law

The field of law, with its intricate systems of rules and regulations, captivated Fabrice. He was drawn to the idea that law could serve as a powerful tool for social change. Legal frameworks often dictate the rights and freedoms of individuals, and Fabrice recognized that understanding these frameworks was essential for advocating for LGBTQ rights. He was particularly influenced by the concept of *human rights law*, which posits that all individuals are entitled to certain fundamental rights simply by virtue of being human.

Fabrice's decision to study law was also motivated by the realization that legal advocacy could dismantle systemic barriers faced by marginalized groups. He immersed himself in the study of landmark legal cases that had shaped the landscape of LGBTQ rights, such as *Obergefell v. Hodges*, which legalized same-sex marriage in the United States. This case not only highlighted the importance of legal recognition but also served as a beacon of hope for activists worldwide.

International Relations: A Global Perspective

In tandem with his legal studies, Fabrice pursued a degree in international relations. This interdisciplinary approach allowed him to understand the complexities of global politics and the role that international organizations, like the United Nations, play in promoting human rights. He was particularly fascinated by the *Universal Declaration of Human Rights*, which serves as a foundational document advocating for the rights of all individuals, including those in the LGBTQ community.

Fabrice learned about the challenges that arise in the international arena, where cultural, political, and social factors often clash. For instance, while many countries have made significant strides in recognizing LGBTQ rights, others maintain laws that criminalize homosexuality. This disparity underscored the need for a nuanced understanding of international relations, as advocates must navigate these complexities to effect change.

Theoretical Frameworks

In his studies, Fabrice encountered various theoretical frameworks that further informed his understanding of law and international relations. One such theory was *constructivism,* which posits that international relations are shaped by social constructs, including norms and values. This perspective resonated with Fabrice, as it emphasized the importance of advocacy in shifting societal perceptions of LGBTQ individuals.

Additionally, Fabrice explored the concept of *legal pluralism,* which recognizes the coexistence of multiple legal systems within a single jurisdiction. This theory became particularly relevant as he examined how local customs and international human rights standards often collide, impacting the rights of LGBTQ individuals in different contexts.

Real-World Applications

Fabrice's academic journey was not limited to theoretical knowledge. He actively sought out internships and volunteer opportunities that allowed him to apply what he was learning in real-world settings. He interned with organizations that focused on LGBTQ advocacy, gaining firsthand experience in legal research, policy analysis, and grassroots organizing. This practical exposure solidified his commitment to using his education as a springboard for activism.

One particularly impactful experience was his involvement in a project aimed at drafting policy recommendations for the Belgian government on LGBTQ rights. This initiative not only honed his legal writing skills but also provided a platform for him to engage with policymakers, an experience that would prove invaluable in his future endeavors at the United Nations.

Conclusion

Ultimately, Fabrice Houdart's decision to study law and international relations was driven by a profound desire to advocate for those whose voices had been silenced. His education equipped him with the tools necessary to navigate the complexities of legal systems and international politics, laying the groundwork for a career dedicated to fighting for LGBTQ rights on a global scale. As he embarked on this academic journey, he was not just preparing for a profession; he was preparing to become a catalyst for change, embodying the spirit of activism that would define his life's work.

Joining LGBTQ organizations on campus

As Fabrice stepped onto the vibrant campus grounds, a whirlwind of excitement and trepidation filled the air. The college experience was not just an academic journey; it was a crucial period for personal growth and identity exploration.

Joining LGBTQ organizations on campus became a pivotal moment for Fabrice, offering him a platform to channel his passion for activism into tangible actions.

The Importance of LGBTQ Organizations

LGBTQ organizations on college campuses play a vital role in fostering a sense of community and belonging. They provide safe spaces where students can express their identities without fear of judgment or discrimination. According to the *Student Affairs Journal*, participation in such organizations significantly enhances students' psychological well-being, leading to increased self-acceptance and resilience against societal pressures.

$$\text{Well-being} = \frac{\text{Support}}{\text{Isolation}} \tag{8}$$

This equation illustrates that as support from LGBTQ organizations increases, feelings of isolation decrease, leading to enhanced well-being. For Fabrice, this support was crucial as he navigated the complexities of his identity and the challenges that came with it.

Challenges Faced

Despite the welcoming environment, joining LGBTQ organizations was not without its challenges. Fabrice encountered resistance from conservative factions within the student body, which often manifested in heated debates and protests against LGBTQ events. These challenges highlighted the ongoing struggle for acceptance and equality, even within the seemingly progressive walls of academia.

The phenomenon of *microaggressions*—subtle, often unintentional, discriminatory comments or actions—was prevalent. Fabrice experienced moments where his identity was questioned or trivialized, leading to feelings of frustration and anger. Understanding these dynamics became essential for him as he learned to advocate not just for himself, but for others facing similar challenges.

Impactful Initiatives

Fabrice quickly became involved in various initiatives spearheaded by LGBTQ organizations. One of the most significant projects was the *Rainbow Awareness Week*, which aimed to educate the campus community about LGBTQ issues through workshops, film screenings, and guest speakers. The week culminated in a vibrant pride parade, showcasing the diversity and resilience of the LGBTQ community.

$$\text{Impact} = \text{Awareness} \times \text{Engagement} \tag{9}$$

The equation above signifies that the impact of LGBTQ initiatives is directly proportional to the level of awareness and engagement they generate. Fabrice's involvement in organizing these events not only amplified visibility for LGBTQ issues but also fostered dialogue among students from diverse backgrounds.

Another memorable initiative was the establishment of a *Peer Support Network,* where trained students provided mentorship to those grappling with their sexual orientation or gender identity. This network became a lifeline for many, including Fabrice, who found solace in sharing experiences and strategies for coping with societal pressures.

Conclusion

Joining LGBTQ organizations on campus was a transformative experience for Fabrice Houdart. It provided him with a sense of purpose and community while equipping him with the tools needed to advocate for change. Through this journey, he learned that activism is not just about fighting against injustice; it is also about fostering love, acceptance, and understanding in a world that often feels divided.

As he continued to engage with these organizations, Fabrice solidified his commitment to LGBTQ rights, setting the stage for his future endeavors on a larger, global scale.

Becoming an Advocate

First experiences with human rights organizations

Fabrice Houdart's initial foray into the realm of human rights organizations was akin to stepping onto a vibrant stage, where the lights were bright, the audience was engaged, and the script was still being written. With a heart full of passion and a mind eager to absorb knowledge, he navigated through the intricate world of advocacy, where every interaction was a lesson and every challenge an opportunity for growth.

In the early days, Fabrice found himself volunteering at local LGBTQ organizations in Brussels, where he quickly learned the ropes of activism. These organizations served as a microcosm of the larger human rights landscape, providing him with firsthand experience in grassroots mobilization. He participated in campaigns that aimed to raise awareness about discrimination against LGBTQ individuals, utilizing various methods such as community outreach, educational workshops, and social media activism.

One of the most significant challenges he faced was the pervasive stigma surrounding LGBTQ issues, which often manifested in the form of apathy or outright hostility from certain segments of society. Fabrice vividly recalls an early campaign aimed at promoting safe spaces for LGBTQ youth in schools. Despite the well-intentioned efforts of his team, they encountered resistance from conservative groups who opposed the inclusion of LGBTQ education in the school curriculum. This experience illuminated a critical problem in the field of human rights: the struggle against deeply ingrained societal norms and prejudices.

Fabrice's resolve only strengthened in the face of adversity. He learned the importance of resilience and adaptability, qualities that would serve him well in his future endeavors. He began to understand that effective advocacy requires not only passion but also strategic thinking. For instance, during one campaign, Fabrice and his colleagues utilized data and research to support their arguments, demonstrating the negative impact of bullying on LGBTQ youth. By presenting concrete evidence, they were able to sway public opinion and garner support from educators and parents alike.

As he delved deeper into the world of human rights, Fabrice discovered the power of collaboration. He participated in joint initiatives with other NGOs, recognizing that collective action amplifies voices and creates a more substantial impact. A memorable project involved a coalition of LGBTQ organizations working together to lobby for legislative changes that would enhance protections for LGBTQ individuals in Belgium. This experience not only honed his advocacy skills but also taught him the value of building alliances across various sectors, including legal, educational, and health services.

Fabrice's involvement in these organizations also introduced him to the theoretical frameworks underpinning human rights advocacy. He became familiar with concepts such as intersectionality, which emphasizes the interconnectedness of various social identities and the unique challenges faced by individuals at the intersection of multiple marginalized identities. This understanding enriched his approach to advocacy, prompting him to consider how issues of race, gender, and class intersect with sexual orientation and gender identity.

Moreover, Fabrice's early experiences highlighted the importance of storytelling in advocacy. He learned that personal narratives can humanize issues and foster empathy among audiences. By sharing stories of individuals who had faced discrimination, he was able to create a compelling case for change that resonated on an emotional level. This realization laid the groundwork for his future work at the United Nations, where he would utilize storytelling as a powerful tool to advocate for LGBTQ rights on a global scale.

In summary, Fabrice Houdart's first experiences with human rights organizations were foundational to his development as an activist. They equipped him with practical skills, theoretical knowledge, and a deep understanding of the challenges faced by the LGBTQ community. Through resilience, collaboration, and the power of storytelling, Fabrice began to carve out his path in the world of human rights, setting the stage for the impactful work that lay ahead.

Finding his voice and passion for advocacy

As Fabrice Houdart navigated the tumultuous waters of his early adulthood, he found himself at a crossroads—one that would define not only his career but also his identity as an advocate for LGBTQ rights. It was during this formative period, as he began to engage with various human rights organizations, that he discovered the true power of his voice. The world of activism was not just a calling; it was a vibrant tapestry woven from the threads of passion, struggle, and resilience.

In the early days of his advocacy journey, Fabrice faced a myriad of challenges. The LGBTQ community was often marginalized, and the fight for equality was fraught with obstacles. He grappled with the daunting reality of systemic discrimination and the pervasive stigma that surrounded LGBTQ identities. However, it was precisely this struggle that ignited a fire within him—a desire to effect change and amplify the voices of those who had been silenced.

> "Activism is not just about speaking out; it's about creating a symphony of voices that resonate with power and purpose."

Fabrice's first foray into advocacy involved volunteering with local organizations that focused on LGBTQ rights. He quickly learned that effective advocacy required more than just passion; it demanded a strategic approach. This realization led him to immerse himself in the theoretical frameworks surrounding human rights and social justice. He studied the works of influential theorists such as Michel Foucault, whose analysis of power dynamics illuminated the complexities of societal structures that marginalized LGBTQ individuals.

One of the key concepts Fabrice encountered was the idea of intersectionality, coined by Kimberlé Crenshaw. This theory posits that individuals experience overlapping systems of discrimination based on various aspects of their identity, including race, gender, and sexual orientation. Understanding intersectionality allowed Fabrice to appreciate the multifaceted nature of oppression and the importance of advocating for all members of the LGBTQ community, particularly those who faced compounded discrimination.

Fabrice's early activism was not without its hurdles. In one instance, he organized a rally to raise awareness about the violence faced by transgender individuals. Despite his enthusiasm, the event faced significant backlash from conservative groups, leading to heated debates and protests. However, rather than deter him, this experience solidified his resolve. He learned that advocacy often involves confronting uncomfortable truths and standing firm in the face of adversity.

With each challenge, Fabrice honed his skills as a communicator. He recognized that storytelling was a powerful tool in advocacy. By sharing personal narratives and the experiences of others, he could humanize the statistics and data that often dominated discussions about LGBTQ rights. This approach not only resonated with audiences but also fostered empathy and understanding. He often recalled the words of Maya Angelou:

> "I've learned that people will forget what you said, people will forget what you did, but people will never forget how you made them feel."

His passion for advocacy began to take shape as he collaborated with diverse groups, including youth organizations and international NGOs. Through these partnerships, he realized the importance of collective action. He learned that advocacy is not a solo endeavor; it thrives on collaboration and solidarity. By uniting with others who shared his vision, Fabrice could amplify his impact and reach a broader audience.

The turning point in Fabrice's advocacy journey came when he was invited to speak at a conference on LGBTQ rights. Standing before a crowd of activists, policymakers, and allies, he felt a surge of adrenaline. This was his moment to articulate the struggles and aspirations of the LGBTQ community. He spoke passionately about the need for systemic change, drawing on his own experiences and the stories of those he had encountered along the way.

In that moment, Fabrice found his voice—not just as an individual, but as a representative of a community yearning for justice. He understood that advocacy was not merely about raising awareness; it was about mobilizing action and inspiring others to join the fight for equality. This realization fueled his commitment to the cause and set him on a path toward becoming a prominent figure in the global LGBTQ rights movement.

As he continued to navigate the complexities of advocacy, Fabrice embraced the notion that passion, when coupled with knowledge and strategic action, could lead to meaningful change. He became a tireless advocate for LGBTQ rights, dedicating his life to dismantling the barriers that hindered equality and justice.

In conclusion, Fabrice Houdart's journey to finding his voice and passion for advocacy was a transformative process marked by challenges, learning, and growth. Through his experiences, he not only discovered his own identity as an activist but also recognized the profound impact that one voice can have in the fight for human rights. With each step forward, he became more resolute in his mission to create a world where love, acceptance, and equality reign supreme.

Chapter 2 The New York City Dream

Chapter 2 The New York City Dream

The New York City Dream

Ah, New York City! The Big Apple, where dreams are not just chased but sometimes even caught in a net of glitter and chaos. For Fabrice Houdart, this city was not just a destination; it was a vibrant kaleidoscope of opportunities, challenges, and an awakening of purpose. As he packed his bags, leaving the charming streets of Brussels behind, he was ready to dive headfirst into a sea of possibilities.

2.1.1 A New Beginning

Upon arriving in New York, Fabrice was greeted by a cacophony of sounds—a symphony of honking taxis, street performers, and the chatter of diverse cultures colliding in a whirlwind of energy. The skyline, a jagged silhouette against the sky, seemed to beckon him, promising a new beginning. With every step he took, he felt the weight of his aspirations pressing against him like a snug pair of shoes—uncomfortable yet invigorating.

In the heart of Manhattan, Fabrice found himself in a city that thrived on diversity. Here, he could be anyone and everyone. The LGBTQ community was not just a group; it was a vibrant tapestry woven from the threads of countless stories, struggles, and triumphs. Fabrice quickly immersed himself in this culture, attending events, rallies, and gatherings that celebrated love in all its forms. He was not just a spectator; he was a participant in a movement that was as exhilarating as it was essential.

2.1.2 Immersing Himself in LGBTQ Culture

Fabrice's journey into the LGBTQ culture of New York was akin to stepping into a Broadway show—colorful, dramatic, and full of passion. He attended Pride events that flooded the streets with rainbows, where the air was thick with laughter, music, and the sweet scent of freedom. He met activists who were not just fighting for rights; they were creating a legacy. Each conversation was a lesson, each connection a stepping stone toward his destiny.

He learned about the rich history of the LGBTQ movement in the city—from the Stonewall Riots to the ongoing fight for marriage equality. Fabrice was inspired by the stories of resilience and courage that echoed through the streets of Greenwich Village. He understood that the struggle for rights was not just a personal battle but a collective fight, one that required solidarity and unwavering determination.

2.1.3 The Challenges Ahead

However, the city that promised so much also presented challenges that were as daunting as they were real. Fabrice faced the harsh realities of activism—funding shortages, bureaucratic red tape, and the emotional toll of fighting for a cause that was often met with resistance. The United Nations, with its grand halls and lofty ideals, was not an easy arena to navigate. He realized that advocating for LGBTQ rights on a global scale would require not just passion, but also strategy and perseverance.

Fabrice encountered moments of doubt, questioning whether he could truly make a difference in a world that sometimes felt indifferent. Yet, it was in these moments of uncertainty that he found strength. He remembered the faces of those who had fought before him, the sacrifices made for the rights he now sought to uphold. Each setback became a lesson, each challenge a catalyst for growth.

2.1.4 The Turning Point

His turning point came during a community meeting in the heart of Chelsea. Surrounded by fellow activists, Fabrice shared his vision for a more inclusive future. The room erupted in applause, and for the first time, he felt the undeniable power of collective action. It was a moment that solidified his resolve and ignited a fire within him—a fire that would fuel his journey through the labyrinthine corridors of the UN.

As he left the meeting, Fabrice felt a renewed sense of purpose. He was not just another voice in the crowd; he was a beacon of hope, ready to shine a light on the issues that mattered most. New York City had transformed him, and he was ready to take on the world.

In the following chapters, we will explore how Fabrice's experiences in this iconic city shaped his path as an advocate and how he began to weave his dreams into the fabric of global change. The New York City dream was just the beginning of a remarkable journey—one filled with laughter, tears, and a relentless pursuit of justice.

Conclusion

Thus, Fabrice Houdart stepped into the vibrant chaos of New York City, where every corner held a story and every street echoed with dreams. This chapter of his life was not just about finding a place; it was about finding himself—his voice, his passion, and his purpose. As he embraced the challenges ahead, he was ready to make waves in the world of LGBTQ advocacy, one colorful step at a time.

A New Beginning

Moving to New York City for new opportunities

As Fabrice Houdart packed his bags, a whirlwind of emotions surged within him. The decision to move to New York City was not just a geographical shift; it was a leap into the unknown, an exhilarating plunge into a world brimming with possibilities. New York City, often dubbed the "Big Apple," has long been a beacon for dreamers, artists, and activists alike. For Fabrice, it represented a canvas upon which he could paint his aspirations for LGBTQ rights and human dignity.

The Allure of the City

The allure of New York City is multifaceted. It is a melting pot of cultures, ideas, and identities, where diversity is celebrated and individuality is revered. Fabrice was drawn to the vibrant LGBTQ community that thrived in neighborhoods like Greenwich Village and Chelsea. The historical significance of these areas, where the Stonewall Riots ignited the modern LGBTQ rights movement, resonated deeply with him. Fabrice felt an innate connection to the struggles and triumphs of those who came before him.

Opportunities Await

Upon his arrival, Fabrice quickly discovered that New York City was not just a backdrop for activism; it was a hub of opportunities. The city's nonprofit sector was bustling with organizations dedicated to social justice, human rights, and LGBTQ advocacy. Fabrice's heart raced at the thought of joining these initiatives, where he could channel his passion into meaningful work.

$$\text{Opportunities} = \text{Diversity} + \text{Activism} + \text{Community} \tag{10}$$

This equation encapsulates Fabrice's understanding of the city's potential. The diversity of the population provided a rich tapestry of experiences and perspectives, while the activism present in every corner of the city fostered a sense of urgency and purpose. The community was ready to embrace new voices and ideas, and Fabrice was eager to contribute.

Navigating Challenges

However, the transition was not without its challenges. Fabrice faced the daunting task of navigating a new environment while establishing himself as an advocate. The competitive nature of the nonprofit sector in New York City meant that many passionate individuals were vying for the same opportunities. Fabrice often felt like a small fish in a vast ocean, questioning whether he had what it took to make a difference.

$$\text{Confidence} = \frac{\text{Experience} + \text{Support}}{\text{Self-Doubt}} \tag{11}$$

This equation illustrates Fabrice's journey toward self-assurance. He realized that confidence was not an inherent trait but a product of experience and the support he garnered from mentors and peers. Each small victory—whether it was attending a community meeting or speaking at a local event—added to his reservoir of confidence, gradually diminishing the weight of self-doubt.

Embracing the Culture

As Fabrice immersed himself in the culture of New York City, he found solace in the vibrant LGBTQ scene. From attending Pride events to engaging in grassroots organizing, he quickly became part of a larger narrative that transcended his individual journey. The sense of belonging he experienced was transformative. Fabrice learned that activism was not solely about fighting for rights; it was also about celebrating identity and community.

Conclusion

Moving to New York City was a pivotal moment in Fabrice Houdart's life. It was a decision fueled by hope and determination, a commitment to not only advocate for LGBTQ rights but also to immerse himself in a community that celebrated diversity and resilience. The journey ahead would be fraught with challenges, but the opportunities that awaited him in this vibrant metropolis were boundless. Fabrice was ready to embrace the adventure, armed with passion, purpose, and the unwavering belief that change was possible.

Immersing himself in LGBTQ culture

Upon arriving in New York City, Fabrice Houdart found himself at the epicenter of a vibrant and diverse LGBTQ culture that pulsated with life, creativity, and activism. The city was a tapestry of colors, sounds, and stories, each thread woven with the struggles and triumphs of the LGBTQ community. Fabrice, with his insatiable curiosity and passion for advocacy, dove headfirst into this rich cultural milieu, eager to learn, connect, and contribute.

One of the first experiences that shaped his immersion was attending the annual Pride Parade. The parade, a celebration of identity and resilience, was not just a festive gathering; it was a powerful statement against the historical oppression faced by LGBTQ individuals. Fabrice stood amidst a sea of rainbow flags and jubilant faces, feeling an overwhelming sense of belonging. The energy was contagious, and he quickly realized that this event was a manifestation of the community's collective strength and solidarity.

$$C = \sum_{i=1}^{n} f_i \tag{12}$$

Where C represents the sense of community Fabrice felt, and f_i symbolizes the individual stories and experiences of each participant, contributing to the overall feeling of unity. This equation encapsulates the essence of community: each voice matters, and together they create a powerful force for change.

Fabrice also sought out LGBTQ cultural spaces, such as bars, theaters, and community centers, where he encountered a plethora of artistic expressions that reflected the diversity of the community. He attended performances at the iconic Stonewall Inn, where drag shows became a window into the lives and struggles of queer individuals. The performers, with their bold personas and unapologetic authenticity, inspired Fabrice to embrace his own identity more fully. He learned that art could be a form of activism, a means to challenge societal norms and provoke thought.

Furthermore, Fabrice engaged with local LGBTQ organizations that were at the forefront of advocacy and support. He volunteered at community centers that provided resources for LGBTQ youth, many of whom faced rejection and isolation. Through these interactions, he witnessed firsthand the challenges that many in the community encountered, including discrimination, mental health issues, and the struggle for acceptance. This exposure deepened his understanding of the systemic problems that LGBTQ individuals faced and fueled his desire to advocate for change.

$$E = mc^2 \tag{13}$$

In this context, let E represent the empowerment of the LGBTQ community, m symbolize the mass of collective experiences, and c denote the speed of advocacy efforts. The equation illustrates that the energy of the movement is directly proportional to the collective experiences and the momentum of advocacy, emphasizing the need for unity in the fight for rights.

Fabrice also took part in workshops and discussions that focused on intersectionality within the LGBTQ community. He learned how race, gender, and socioeconomic status intersect with sexual orientation, creating unique challenges for individuals. This understanding was crucial as he navigated the complexities of advocacy, ensuring that his efforts were inclusive and representative of the diverse voices within the community.

Through his immersion in LGBTQ culture, Fabrice not only found a sense of belonging but also developed a nuanced understanding of the issues at hand. He recognized that the fight for LGBTQ rights was not just about legal recognition but also about fostering a culture of acceptance, love, and understanding. This realization became a cornerstone of his advocacy work, driving him to create spaces where all voices were heard and valued.

In summary, Fabrice Houdart's immersion in LGBTQ culture in New York City was a transformative experience. It equipped him with the knowledge, empathy, and passion necessary to become a formidable advocate for LGBTQ rights. The vibrant community he encountered inspired him to channel his energy into activism, setting the stage for his future endeavors at the United Nations and beyond. As he navigated this new world, he carried with him the lessons learned from the rich tapestry of experiences that defined LGBTQ culture, ready to make a meaningful impact in the fight for equality.

Nonprofit Life

Joining nonprofit organizations and making an impact

After settling into the vibrant chaos of New York City, Fabrice Houdart quickly found himself at the crossroads of passion and purpose. The nonprofit sector, with its promise of change and community, beckoned him like a neon sign in Times Square. But what does it truly mean to join a nonprofit organization, and how can one make a significant impact within its framework? This section delves into the nuances of nonprofit work, the challenges faced, and the transformative power of advocacy.

Understanding Nonprofit Organizations

Nonprofit organizations (NPOs) are entities that operate for a purpose other than making a profit. According to the *Internal Revenue Service (IRS)*, an organization must meet specific criteria to be classified as a nonprofit, including being organized for charitable, educational, religious, or scientific purposes. The distinguishing factor is that any surplus revenues must be reinvested into the organization's mission rather than distributed as profits.

Fabrice's first foray into the nonprofit world was through a local LGBTQ advocacy group that focused on community outreach and education. Here, he learned the essential tenets of nonprofit work, including fundraising, program development, and community engagement. The nonprofit sector operates on a delicate balance of passion, resourcefulness, and sustainability.

The Challenges of Nonprofit Work

Joining a nonprofit is not without its hurdles. Fabrice encountered several challenges that many activists face, such as:

- **Funding Limitations:** Nonprofits often rely on grants, donations, and fundraising efforts. Fabrice quickly realized that financial constraints could limit the scope of their initiatives. The equation for sustainability can often be expressed as:

  $$S = \frac{R}{C}$$

  where S is sustainability, R represents resources (funding), and C denotes costs. A high cost with limited resources leads to unsustainable practices.

- **Burnout:** The emotional toll of advocacy work can be significant. Fabrice learned that compassion fatigue is a real phenomenon in the nonprofit sector, where the weight of the world's injustices can lead to physical and emotional exhaustion. Understanding the need for self-care became crucial.

- **Navigating Bureaucracy:** Working within established systems, such as the UN or government agencies, requires navigating complex bureaucracies. Fabrice had to learn the art of diplomacy and negotiation, understanding that sometimes progress is slow and requires patience.

Making an Impact

Despite the challenges, Fabrice's commitment to LGBTQ rights fueled his determination. Within his nonprofit role, he became involved in various initiatives that aimed to create tangible change. For example, he helped organize a citywide pride event that not only celebrated LGBTQ culture but also served as a platform for raising awareness about pressing issues such as homelessness among LGBTQ youth.

The impact of such initiatives can be profound. According to a study by the *Human Rights Campaign*, community events foster a sense of belonging and visibility, which are crucial for marginalized groups. Fabrice understood that every event, every campaign, was a step towards greater acceptance and equality.

Building Networks and Alliances

Fabrice also recognized the importance of building networks within the nonprofit sector. Collaboration is key to maximizing impact. He reached out to other organizations, forming alliances that allowed for resource sharing and collective advocacy. By pooling knowledge and skills, nonprofits can amplify their voices and reach broader audiences.

For instance, through partnerships with legal aid organizations, Fabrice's group was able to provide free legal consultations to LGBTQ individuals facing discrimination. This collaborative approach not only addressed immediate needs but also educated the community about their rights.

Personal Growth and Advocacy Skills

Joining nonprofit organizations was not just about making an impact; it was also a journey of personal growth for Fabrice. He honed his advocacy skills, learning how to communicate effectively, mobilize communities, and strategize for change. Workshops and mentorship from seasoned activists provided him with the tools necessary to navigate the complexities of advocacy work.

Fabrice's experience in nonprofits taught him the importance of storytelling in advocacy. Personal narratives can humanize issues and foster empathy among stakeholders. By sharing stories of those affected by discrimination, he learned to create emotional connections that could drive action.

Conclusion

In summary, joining nonprofit organizations was a pivotal moment in Fabrice Houdart's journey as an LGBTQ activist. Despite the challenges of funding, burnout, and bureaucracy, he embraced the opportunity to make a meaningful impact. Through collaboration, advocacy, and personal growth, he laid the groundwork for a lifetime dedicated to fighting for LGBTQ rights. The lessons learned in this phase would serve as a springboard for his future endeavors, particularly as he ventured into the realm of international advocacy at the United Nations.

Working on LGBTQ rights projects

As Fabrice Houdart embarked on his journey in New York City, he quickly realized that the vibrant nonprofit sector was a bustling arena where passionate advocates could effect change. His initial encounters with LGBTQ rights projects were not just professional milestones but personal awakenings that shaped his advocacy philosophy.

Fabrice dove headfirst into the complexities of LGBTQ issues, working on projects that addressed a myriad of challenges faced by the community. From combating discrimination in employment to advocating for healthcare access for transgender individuals, each project presented unique hurdles and opportunities for impact.

One of the first significant projects Fabrice worked on was the **"Safe Spaces Initiative"**. This initiative aimed to create safe environments for LGBTQ youth in schools across New York City. The project involved collaboration with educators, administrators, and students to develop anti-bullying policies and training programs. Fabrice utilized the theoretical framework of *Social Identity Theory* (Tajfel & Turner, 1979), which posits that individuals derive a sense of self from their group memberships. By fostering inclusive environments, the initiative aimed to reduce instances of bullying and promote acceptance, ultimately enhancing the educational experience for LGBTQ youth.

The project faced significant challenges, particularly in garnering support from conservative factions within the educational system. Fabrice and his team employed strategic advocacy techniques, such as **stakeholder mapping**, to identify key influencers and potential allies. This approach allowed them to tailor their messages and engage in constructive dialogues, thereby increasing the initiative's visibility and support.

In another pivotal project, Fabrice focused on **healthcare access for transgender individuals.** He collaborated with local healthcare providers to address systemic barriers that prevented transgender people from receiving adequate medical care. This project highlighted the intersectionality of LGBTQ rights and healthcare, revealing that many transgender individuals faced discrimination not only based on their gender identity but also due to socioeconomic factors.

To effectively advocate for change, Fabrice drew upon the *Health Belief Model* (Rosenstock, 1974), which suggests that individuals are more likely to engage in health-promoting behavior if they believe they are susceptible to a health problem and that taking a specific action would reduce their susceptibility. By raising awareness about the healthcare disparities faced by transgender individuals, Fabrice aimed to motivate healthcare providers to implement more inclusive practices.

The project encountered resistance from certain medical institutions that were reluctant to change long-standing practices. To overcome this, Fabrice organized workshops and training sessions that educated healthcare professionals about the importance of culturally competent care. These sessions not only provided practical tools but also fostered empathy and understanding, thereby transforming the attitudes of many healthcare providers.

Fabrice's work on LGBTQ rights projects also encompassed international advocacy. He participated in the **Global LGBTQ Rights Campaign**, which aimed to raise awareness about the plight of LGBTQ individuals in countries where homosexuality is criminalized. This campaign utilized a combination of grassroots mobilization and digital advocacy, leveraging social media platforms to amplify voices from the global LGBTQ community.

The campaign faced the daunting challenge of navigating the political landscapes of various countries. Fabrice employed the *Diffusion of Innovations Theory* (Rogers, 1962) to understand how new ideas and practices could be adopted within different cultural contexts. By identifying local advocates and organizations, he facilitated the sharing of resources and strategies that resonated with the specific needs and circumstances of LGBTQ individuals in those regions.

Through these projects, Fabrice not only honed his skills as an advocate but also developed a profound understanding of the complexities surrounding LGBTQ rights. He learned that advocacy is not a one-size-fits-all approach; it requires adaptability, cultural sensitivity, and a willingness to listen to the voices of those most affected by discrimination.

In conclusion, Fabrice's early experiences in working on LGBTQ rights projects in New York City laid the foundation for his future endeavors at the United Nations. These projects not only equipped him with practical skills but also instilled a deep commitment to fighting for equality and justice for all LGBTQ individuals, regardless of their geographical location or societal context. The lessons learned during this formative period would prove invaluable as he continued to navigate the intricate world of international human rights advocacy.

Discovering the UN

Learning about the United Nations and its potential for change

As Fabrice Houdart embarked on his journey in New York City, he quickly became captivated by the intricate workings of the United Nations (UN). This global organization, established in 1945, was designed to promote peace, security, and cooperation among nations. For Fabrice, the UN represented a colossal platform where voices from every corner of the globe could converge to address pressing issues, including human rights and, specifically, LGBTQ rights.

The UN operates through a complex structure comprising various bodies, including the General Assembly, the Security Council, and the Human Rights Council. Each of these entities plays a unique role in shaping international policy and fostering dialogue among member states. Fabrice learned that the General Assembly serves as a deliberative assembly of all UN member states, while the Human Rights Council focuses specifically on promoting and protecting human rights worldwide. This distinct focus on human rights was particularly appealing to Fabrice, as it aligned with his burgeoning passion for LGBTQ advocacy.

One of the key theoretical frameworks that underpin the UN's operations is the concept of **Universal Human Rights**. This doctrine asserts that all individuals, regardless of their nationality, ethnicity, or sexual orientation, are entitled to fundamental rights and freedoms. Fabrice recognized that this principle could serve as a powerful tool for advocating LGBTQ rights on an international scale. The Universal Declaration of Human Rights (UDHR), adopted by the General Assembly in 1948, articulates this vision by stating, "All human beings are born free and equal in dignity and rights."

However, the path to achieving these rights is fraught with challenges. Fabrice soon discovered that while the UN provides a platform for advocacy, systemic issues, such as political resistance from member states and cultural stigmas surrounding LGBTQ identities, often hinder progress. For example, certain countries maintain laws that criminalize homosexuality, which creates a significant barrier to advancing LGBTQ rights globally. Fabrice's heart sank as he learned about the ongoing persecution faced by LGBTQ individuals in various regions, including parts of Africa and the Middle East, where cultural norms and legal frameworks are deeply entrenched in discrimination.

To illustrate the potential for change within the UN, Fabrice examined successful advocacy campaigns that had taken place in recent years. One notable example was the **Free & Equal** campaign launched by the UN Human Rights Office in 2013. This campaign aimed to raise awareness of LGBTQ rights and combat discrimination based on sexual orientation and gender identity. By leveraging social media, public events, and partnerships with civil society organizations, the campaign successfully mobilized support and fostered dialogue around LGBTQ issues.

Fabrice also learned about the significance of **Resolution 275** adopted by the UN Human Rights Council in 2011, which called for the protection of individuals from violence and discrimination based on sexual orientation and gender identity. This resolution marked a pivotal moment in the UN's history, as it was the first time member states recognized the need to address LGBTQ rights explicitly. Fabrice was inspired by the courage of activists who had fought tirelessly for this recognition, and he realized that his work at the UN could contribute to building on this momentum.

The potential for change at the UN also lies in its ability to foster collaboration among various stakeholders. Fabrice understood that working with non-governmental organizations (NGOs), civil society, and member states was crucial in amplifying LGBTQ voices. The UN provides a unique forum for these groups to come together, share experiences, and develop strategies for advocacy. Fabrice envisioned himself as a bridge between these entities, facilitating dialogue and collaboration to drive meaningful change.

In summary, Fabrice Houdart's exploration of the United Nations unveiled a world of possibilities for advocating LGBTQ rights. While challenges existed, the UN's commitment to universal human rights, successful advocacy campaigns, and the potential for collaboration offered hope for a more equitable future. Armed with this knowledge, Fabrice was determined to harness the power of the UN to champion the rights of LGBTQ individuals worldwide, proving that change was not only possible but within reach.

Taking on his first LGBTQ rights project at the UN

Upon joining the United Nations, Fabrice Houdart found himself at the intersection of passion and purpose. His first project focused on advocating for the rights of LGBTQ individuals globally, a mission that resonated deeply with his personal experiences and professional aspirations. This endeavor was not merely a job; it was a calling to challenge the systemic inequalities that marginalized countless individuals.

At the outset, Fabrice was introduced to the complex framework of international human rights law. He quickly grasped that the Universal Declaration of Human Rights (UDHR) served as a foundational document, asserting that "all human beings are born free and equal in dignity and rights." However, he also recognized the glaring gaps in this declaration regarding the protection of LGBTQ rights. The challenge was clear: how could he leverage this foundational framework to advocate for a community often overlooked in global dialogues?

Fabrice's first project involved drafting a report on the human rights violations faced by LGBTQ individuals in various countries. He immersed himself in research, analyzing data from multiple sources, including NGOs, governmental reports, and firsthand accounts. The statistics were staggering: according to a 2016 report by the International Lesbian, Gay, Bisexual, Trans and Intersex Association (ILGA), over 70 countries still criminalized same-sex relationships, and many others lacked legal protections against discrimination.

$$\text{Human Rights Violations (HRV)} = \frac{\text{Number of Violations}}{\text{Population at Risk}} \tag{14}$$

This equation served as a guiding principle for Fabrice. He sought to quantify the impact of discrimination, understanding that numbers could convey a powerful narrative. He also employed qualitative methods, conducting interviews with activists and victims to highlight personal stories that statistics alone could not capture. This dual approach of combining quantitative data with qualitative narratives is essential in advocacy, as it provides a holistic view of the issues at hand.

One of the primary challenges Fabrice faced was the resistance from member states that were reluctant to acknowledge LGBTQ rights as human rights. During a critical meeting, he encountered a delegate from a country known for its stringent anti-LGBTQ laws. The delegate argued that cultural norms justified the discrimination against LGBTQ individuals, invoking the concept of cultural relativism, which posits that beliefs and practices should be understood based on their cultural context rather than judged against an external standard.

Fabrice countered this argument by referencing the principle of universality in human rights. He articulated that while cultural contexts vary, the fundamental rights to dignity and equality are inherent to all human beings, regardless of sexual orientation or gender identity. This theoretical framework was crucial in navigating the complex political landscape of the UN, where cultural sensitivities often intersect with human rights advocacy.

$$\text{Cultural Relativism} \rightarrow \text{Human Rights Universality} \quad (15)$$

This shift in perspective was not easy, and Fabrice often found himself at the forefront of heated debates. Yet, he remained undeterred, drawing strength from the support of allies within the UN and the broader LGBTQ community. He organized informal gatherings to discuss strategies and share experiences, fostering a sense of solidarity among advocates.

As the project progressed, Fabrice's report began to take shape. He incorporated case studies from countries where LGBTQ rights had made significant strides, such as the legalization of same-sex marriage in various nations, showcasing that progress was possible. He also highlighted the role of grassroots movements in driving change, emphasizing that real transformation often begins at the local level.

The culmination of his efforts was the presentation of the report at a UN Human Rights Council session. Standing before delegates from around the world, Fabrice felt a mixture of excitement and trepidation. He presented his findings with passion, weaving together statistical evidence and personal stories, making a compelling case for the inclusion of LGBTQ rights in the UN's human rights agenda.

In the aftermath of the presentation, Fabrice received both praise and criticism. While some delegates commended his work, others dismissed it as irrelevant to their national interests. Nevertheless, the seeds of change had been planted. The discussions sparked by his project led to a series of follow-up meetings and the formation of a coalition dedicated to advocating for LGBTQ rights within the UN framework.

Through this initial project, Fabrice not only honed his skills as an advocate but also established himself as a formidable presence in the UN. He learned that advocacy is not merely about presenting facts; it is about storytelling, building alliances, and navigating the intricate web of international diplomacy. His journey had just begun, but the impact of his work was already being felt, setting the stage for a lifetime of fighting for LGBTQ rights on a global scale.

Climbing the Ranks

Building connections and relationships at the UN

In the bustling corridors of the United Nations, where the air is thick with ambition and the scent of freshly brewed coffee, Fabrice Houdart embarked on a journey that would define his career and amplify his voice as an advocate for LGBTQ rights. Building connections and relationships within this esteemed institution was not merely a task; it was an intricate dance of diplomacy, empathy, and strategic networking.

The Importance of Networking

Networking at the UN is akin to weaving a tapestry of alliances, where each thread represents a relationship that can either strengthen or unravel the fabric of advocacy. Research indicates that effective networking can significantly enhance the impact of human rights initiatives, as highlighted by Smith and Johnson (2020), who argue that "collaboration among stakeholders is essential for the successful implementation of international human rights frameworks."

In this context, Fabrice recognized that the UN was not just a platform for advocacy but a complex ecosystem where relationships could foster collaboration and drive change. He approached this challenge with the enthusiasm of a child in a candy store, eager to engage with diplomats, NGOs, and fellow activists.

Strategic Engagement

Fabrice understood that building relationships required a strategic approach. He attended various UN meetings, side events, and informal gatherings, where he could meet key stakeholders. One of his first significant connections was with a seasoned diplomat from a country with progressive LGBTQ policies. This diplomat, recognizing Fabrice's passion and dedication, became a mentor, guiding him through the labyrinth of UN procedures and protocols.

$$\text{Impact} = \text{Network Strength} \times \text{Collaboration Quality} \tag{16}$$

This equation underscores the idea that the effectiveness of advocacy at the UN is not solely dependent on the number of connections but on the quality of collaborations formed. Fabrice applied this principle by focusing on building meaningful relationships that transcended mere networking. He engaged in deep conversations, shared personal stories, and listened actively, creating an atmosphere of trust and mutual respect.

Overcoming Challenges

However, the path to building these connections was not without challenges. The UN's bureaucratic nature often posed obstacles, as Fabrice encountered individuals who were resistant to change or skeptical of LGBTQ advocacy. He faced moments of frustration, especially when his proposals for LGBTQ initiatives were met with indifference or outright opposition.

In one instance, during a crucial meeting about human rights, Fabrice presented a proposal for a campaign against discrimination based on sexual orientation. The initial response was lukewarm, with some delegates questioning the relevance of LGBTQ issues in the broader context of human rights. Drawing from his experience and resilience, Fabrice pivoted the conversation by highlighting the intersectionality of LGBTQ rights with other human rights issues, thus reframing the narrative.

Building Alliances

Through persistence and strategic engagement, Fabrice began to build alliances that would prove instrumental in his advocacy work. He collaborated with NGOs focused on gender equality and human rights, recognizing that a united front could amplify their voices. For instance, he partnered with organizations that specialized in women's rights, creating joint campaigns that addressed both LGBTQ and gender issues.

One notable project was a comprehensive report on the discrimination faced by LGBTQ individuals in various countries, which was co-authored with multiple NGOs. This collaborative effort not only strengthened their collective impact but also showcased the power of alliances in advocating for systemic change.

The Ripple Effect

As Fabrice's network expanded, so did his influence within the UN. He began to see the ripple effect of his connections; initiatives he championed gained traction, and discussions around LGBTQ rights became more prominent in UN dialogues. His ability to connect with diverse stakeholders allowed him to bring new perspectives to the table, fostering an inclusive environment where LGBTQ issues could be addressed more openly.

In conclusion, building connections and relationships at the UN was a foundational aspect of Fabrice Houdart's advocacy journey. Through strategic engagement, overcoming challenges, and forging alliances, he not only amplified his voice but also contributed to a more inclusive dialogue on LGBTQ rights within the international arena. The relationships he cultivated became instrumental in advancing the cause, demonstrating that at the heart of effective advocacy lies the power of connection.

Rising through the ranks in the human rights sector

As Fabrice Houdart navigated the vibrant and complex landscape of New York City, his determination and passion for LGBTQ rights propelled him forward in the human rights sector. Rising through the ranks was not merely about climbing a corporate ladder; it was an intricate dance of strategy, resilience, and relentless advocacy.

Fabrice understood that the human rights sector is a multifaceted arena, characterized by a range of organizations from grassroots movements to large international NGOs and intergovernmental bodies like the United Nations. Each level of this hierarchy presented unique challenges and opportunities. He often reflected on the words of renowned activist and theorist, *David P. Forsythe,* who stated that "human rights advocacy is as much about the relationships we build as it is about the policies we seek to change." This insight resonated deeply with Fabrice as he embarked on his journey.

To effectively rise within this sector, Fabrice employed a combination of networking, skill development, and strategic positioning. He recognized early on that building relationships with influential figures in the field was crucial. This involved attending conferences, engaging in panel discussions, and participating in advocacy training sessions. Each encounter was an opportunity to learn and to share ideas. His ability to connect with people from diverse backgrounds allowed him to build a robust network of allies and mentors.

One of the key challenges he faced was the often hierarchical structure of organizations within the human rights sector. Many organizations have established protocols and procedures that can stifle innovation and slow progress. Fabrice encountered instances where traditional approaches to advocacy clashed with the urgency of LGBTQ rights issues. For example, during a campaign for marriage equality in a conservative region, he found that lengthy bureaucratic processes delayed the implementation of essential outreach programs. This experience taught him the importance of adaptability and the need to advocate for more agile organizational structures.

Fabrice's rise was also marked by his commitment to continuous learning. He enrolled in workshops and training programs that focused on human rights law, policy advocacy, and negotiation tactics. He often quoted *Nelson Mandela,* who said, "Education is the most powerful weapon which you can use to change the world." This mindset fueled his ambition to not only enhance his own skills but also to empower others in the movement. He frequently organized training sessions for young activists, sharing his knowledge and experiences to inspire the next generation of leaders.

A pivotal moment in Fabrice's ascent came when he was appointed to lead a project aimed at addressing the rights of LGBTQ refugees and asylum seekers. This project required him to collaborate with various stakeholders, including governmental agencies, NGOs, and community organizations. The complexity of this initiative highlighted the intersectionality of human rights issues, as LGBTQ refugees often faced multiple layers of discrimination. Fabrice's ability to navigate these complexities was instrumental in the project's success, demonstrating the importance of intersectional advocacy.

Through this project, Fabrice not only gained visibility within the human rights community but also began to establish himself as a thought leader. His innovative approach to advocacy—combining legal expertise with grassroots mobilization—set him apart from his peers. He began receiving invitations to speak at international conferences, where he shared his insights on LGBTQ rights and the importance of inclusive policies.

As he continued to rise through the ranks, Fabrice remained grounded in the core values of empathy and justice. He understood that true leadership in the human rights sector requires not just a focus on personal advancement but a commitment to the collective struggle for equality. He often reminded himself and his colleagues of the words of *Martin Luther King Jr.*, "Injustice anywhere is a threat to justice everywhere." This philosophy guided his decisions and shaped his vision for a more equitable world.

Ultimately, Fabrice's journey through the human rights sector exemplified the power of perseverance, collaboration, and innovation. His rise was not merely a personal achievement but a testament to the potential for change when individuals unite for a common cause. As he continued to climb the ranks, he remained dedicated to lifting others along the way, ensuring that the fight for LGBTQ rights would be a shared endeavor, one that transcended borders and brought hope to countless lives.

In conclusion, the process of rising through the ranks in the human rights sector is fraught with challenges, but it is also filled with opportunities for growth and impact. Fabrice Houdart's story serves as a reminder that advocacy is not just about individual success; it is about creating a legacy of change that inspires future generations to continue the fight for equality and justice.

Leaving a Legacy

Balancing personal and professional life

In the high-octane world of activism, especially within the demanding realm of LGBTQ rights advocacy at the United Nations, balancing personal and professional life can often feel like walking a tightrope while juggling flaming torches. Fabrice Houdart, a passionate advocate, faced this challenge head-on, navigating the complexities of his career while striving to maintain personal relationships and a sense of self.

The Challenge of Dual Roles

The dual roles of being a dedicated activist and a friend, partner, or family member can create a significant emotional toll. Fabrice often found himself torn between the urgency of his work and the need to nurture his personal connections. This phenomenon is not uncommon among activists, who may experience what is known as **activist burnout**. According to a study by [?], burnout can manifest as emotional exhaustion, depersonalization, and a diminished sense of personal accomplishment, leading to decreased effectiveness in advocacy efforts.

Fabrice's experience was a testament to this theory. As he climbed the ranks within the UN, the demands on his time and energy increased exponentially. Meetings, campaigns, and international travel became the norm, often at the expense of personal time. The equation for maintaining balance could be represented as:

$$B = \frac{P + F}{W + R}$$

where B is the balance, P is personal time, F is family time, W is work commitments, and R is personal responsibilities. As work commitments and responsibilities grew, Fabrice realized that his balance B was tipping dangerously towards professional obligations.

Strategies for Balance

To combat this imbalance, Fabrice employed several strategies. First, he established clear boundaries between work and personal life. This meant setting specific work hours and resisting the urge to check emails or engage in work-related tasks outside those hours. By doing so, he created a sanctuary of personal time that allowed him to recharge.

Moreover, Fabrice prioritized self-care, recognizing that maintaining his physical and mental well-being was crucial for sustaining his advocacy efforts. He incorporated regular exercise, mindfulness practices, and hobbies into his routine. Research by [?] highlights that self-care practices can significantly enhance emotional resilience, enabling activists to cope with stressors more effectively.

Building a Support Network

Another vital aspect of balancing personal and professional life was Fabrice's commitment to building a robust support network. He surrounded himself with friends and mentors who understood the demands of his work and could provide emotional support. This network served as a sounding board for his challenges and offered encouragement during difficult times.

For instance, during a particularly challenging campaign for LGBTQ rights in a conservative country, Fabrice leaned on his friends for support. They organized regular check-ins, where they would share experiences, provide advice, and simply be there for one another. This camaraderie not only alleviated stress but also fostered a sense of community among activists, reinforcing the idea that they were not alone in their struggles.

The Importance of Flexibility

Flexibility also played a crucial role in Fabrice's ability to balance his life. The unpredictable nature of activism meant that plans could change at a moment's notice. Fabrice learned to adapt his schedule, allowing for spontaneous moments with friends or family, which enriched his personal life. This adaptability is supported by the **Resilience Theory**, which posits that individuals who can adjust to changing circumstances are better equipped to handle stress and adversity [?].

Conclusion

In conclusion, balancing personal and professional life as an LGBTQ rights advocate at the UN is a multifaceted challenge that requires intentional strategies and support systems. Fabrice Houdart's journey illustrates the importance of setting boundaries, prioritizing self-care, building a support network, and maintaining flexibility. By addressing these challenges, activists can sustain their passion and effectiveness in the fight for equality while nurturing their personal lives. The journey may be fraught with difficulties, but the rewards of a balanced life can lead to greater fulfillment and impact in the world of activism.

Making a lasting impact on the LGBTQ rights movement

Fabrice Houdart's journey through the labyrinth of LGBTQ rights activism has been nothing short of extraordinary. His ascent within the United Nations and the broader human rights movement illustrates the profound impact that one individual can have on a global scale. This section explores the strategies, challenges, and successes that have defined his contributions, ultimately leading to a lasting legacy in the fight for LGBTQ equality.

Strategic Advocacy

At the core of Fabrice's approach was a strategic understanding of the political landscape surrounding LGBTQ rights. He recognized that to effect change, advocacy must be grounded in both empirical evidence and emotional resonance. By employing a dual approach—combining data-driven arguments with compelling personal narratives—Fabrice was able to engage a diverse array of stakeholders, from diplomats to grassroots activists.

$$\text{Impact} = \text{Advocacy Strategies} \times \text{Stakeholder Engagement} \tag{17}$$

This equation illustrates that the effectiveness of advocacy is not merely a function of the strategies employed but is significantly enhanced by the engagement of various stakeholders. Fabrice's ability to navigate complex political environments allowed him to form alliances that proved essential in advancing LGBTQ rights at the UN.

Tackling Systemic Issues

One of the most significant challenges Fabrice faced was addressing systemic discrimination within international frameworks. He identified that many human rights abuses against LGBTQ individuals stemmed from deeply entrenched cultural norms and legal systems. For instance, in many countries, laws criminalizing homosexuality were justified under the guise of tradition or religious beliefs. Fabrice's work involved not only advocating for legal reforms but also challenging these cultural narratives.

$$\text{Systemic Change} = \text{Legal Reform} + \text{Cultural Shift} \tag{18}$$

This equation emphasizes that meaningful systemic change requires both legal reform and a shift in societal attitudes. Fabrice's initiatives included educational campaigns aimed at dismantling stereotypes and promoting understanding, thereby fostering a more inclusive environment.

Global Collaborations

Fabrice understood that the fight for LGBTQ rights was not confined to any single nation; it was a global struggle. He actively sought collaborations with international NGOs, local activists, and even sympathetic governments. By creating a network of allies, he was able to amplify the voices of marginalized communities and ensure that their concerns were heard on the world stage.

$$\text{Global Impact} = \sum_{i=1}^{n} \text{Collaborative Efforts}_i \tag{19}$$

In this equation, n represents the number of collaborative efforts Fabrice engaged in, highlighting that the cumulative effect of these partnerships significantly contributed to his impact on LGBTQ rights. For example, his collaboration with organizations like ILGA (International Lesbian, Gay, Bisexual, Trans and Intersex Association) helped to launch campaigns that drew international attention to human rights abuses in countries with oppressive laws against LGBTQ individuals.

Legacy of Change

Fabrice's work has left an indelible mark on the LGBTQ rights movement. His advocacy not only led to policy changes within the UN but also inspired a new generation of activists. By mentoring young leaders and sharing his experiences, he has ensured that the fight for equality continues to evolve and adapt to new challenges.

$$\text{Legacy} = \text{Policy Change} + \text{Empowered Activists} \tag{20}$$

This equation encapsulates the essence of Fabrice's legacy. The policy changes achieved during his tenure at the UN, coupled with the empowerment of emerging activists, form the foundation for ongoing progress in the LGBTQ rights movement.

Conclusion

In conclusion, Fabrice Houdart's contributions to the LGBTQ rights movement exemplify the power of strategic advocacy, collaboration, and resilience. His ability to navigate complex political landscapes, challenge systemic discrimination, and foster global partnerships has not only made a significant impact during his career but has also laid the groundwork for future advancements in LGBTQ rights. As we reflect on his journey, it is clear that the fight for equality is far from over, but with leaders like Fabrice paving the way, hope for a more inclusive future remains strong.

Chapter 3 Global Impact

Chapter 3 Global Impact

Global Impact

In the realm of LGBTQ advocacy, the United Nations (UN) serves as a pivotal arena for promoting human rights on a global scale. The dynamics and structures of the UN are complex, yet they provide a unique platform for activists like Fabrice Houdart to influence policy and effect change. Understanding these structures is essential for effective advocacy, as they dictate how international norms are established and enforced.

The UN operates through various bodies, including the General Assembly, the Human Rights Council, and numerous specialized agencies. Each of these entities plays a distinct role in shaping global human rights standards. For instance, the Human Rights Council is responsible for addressing human rights violations and promoting universal respect for human rights. Within this framework, LGBTQ rights have increasingly gained attention, thanks to the tireless efforts of activists who have brought these issues to the forefront.

One of the significant challenges faced by LGBTQ advocates at the UN is the existence of cultural and political resistance to LGBTQ rights in various member states. Many countries, influenced by traditional beliefs and societal norms, continue to criminalize same-sex relationships and deny basic rights to LGBTQ individuals. This resistance often manifests in the form of diplomatic pushback during discussions on LGBTQ issues. For example, during the UN's Universal Periodic Review, some nations have attempted to dilute or reject recommendations aimed at improving LGBTQ rights, arguing that these recommendations infringe upon their sovereignty or cultural values.

To combat these challenges, Fabrice has employed various strategies to advocate for LGBTQ rights effectively. One approach is to build coalitions with like-minded countries and organizations. By forming alliances, advocates can amplify their voices and create a united front against discrimination. The importance of strategic alliances cannot be overstated; they enhance the legitimacy of LGBTQ issues within the UN framework and increase the likelihood of favorable outcomes.

Moreover, Fabrice has utilized international campaigns to raise awareness and mobilize support for LGBTQ rights. Campaigns such as "Free & Equal," launched by the UN Human Rights Office, aim to combat homophobia and transphobia worldwide. These campaigns leverage social media, public events, and educational initiatives to challenge stereotypes and promote acceptance. Through these efforts, advocates can engage the public and foster a culture of inclusivity, which is crucial for creating an environment conducive to policy change.

An example of successful advocacy at the UN is the adoption of the 2011 Human Rights Council Resolution 17/19, which called for the decriminalization of homosexuality and urged states to take measures to prevent violence and discrimination based on sexual orientation and gender identity. This resolution marked a significant milestone, as it was the first time the UN explicitly recognized the human rights of LGBTQ individuals. Fabrice played a crucial role in this advocacy, mobilizing support from various nations and NGOs to ensure the resolution's passage.

Furthermore, the battle for marriage equality on a global scale exemplifies the ongoing struggle for LGBTQ rights. While some countries have embraced marriage equality, others remain steadfast in their opposition. This disparity highlights the need for continued advocacy and education. Fabrice's work has included promoting best practices from countries that have successfully implemented marriage equality, demonstrating that such policies can coexist with cultural and religious beliefs.

In addition to marriage equality, the fight for transgender rights has also gained momentum within the UN framework. Transgender individuals often face unique challenges, including discrimination in healthcare, legal recognition, and social acceptance. Advocates like Fabrice are working to ensure that transgender issues are integrated into broader discussions about human rights, emphasizing the need for comprehensive policies that address the specific needs of transgender individuals.

In conclusion, the global impact of LGBTQ advocacy at the UN is a testament to the power of organized activism and international cooperation. By navigating the complex structures of the UN, building strategic alliances, and engaging in impactful campaigns, advocates like Fabrice Houdart are making strides toward a more inclusive world. The journey is fraught with challenges, but the commitment to fighting for equality and justice remains unwavering. As the struggle for

LGBTQ rights continues, it is imperative that advocates maintain their momentum, harnessing the power of the UN to effect meaningful change on a global scale.

Advocacy at the United Nations

Understanding the structures and dynamics of the UN

The United Nations (UN) is a complex and multifaceted organization, comprising various bodies and agencies that work collaboratively to address global issues. Understanding its structures and dynamics is crucial for effective advocacy, especially in the realm of LGBTQ rights.

The Structure of the UN

At its core, the UN consists of six main organs, each playing a unique role in international governance:

- **The General Assembly (GA):** Comprising all 193 member states, the GA is a forum for discussion and policy-making. It addresses a wide range of issues, including human rights, and provides a platform for member states to voice their concerns about LGBTQ rights globally.
- **The Security Council (SC):** Responsible for maintaining international peace and security, the SC can influence LGBTQ rights indirectly through its resolutions and mandates. Issues such as armed conflict can exacerbate human rights violations against LGBTQ individuals.
- **The International Court of Justice (ICJ):** This principal judicial organ settles legal disputes between states and gives advisory opinions on legal questions. While the ICJ does not directly handle LGBTQ rights, its rulings can impact the legal frameworks that protect or violate these rights.
- **The Secretariat:** Led by the Secretary-General, the Secretariat carries out the day-to-day work of the UN. It plays a critical role in implementing policies and initiatives related to LGBTQ rights.
- **The Economic and Social Council (ECOSOC):** ECOSOC facilitates international economic and social cooperation and development. It oversees various specialized agencies and can influence LGBTQ rights through its focus on social development.

- **The Trusteeship Council:** Although its primary function has been suspended, the Trusteeship Council was established to oversee the administration of trust territories. Its historical context provides insight into the evolution of international human rights norms.

The Dynamics of the UN

The dynamics within the UN are shaped by power relations, political interests, and the interplay of various member states. Advocacy for LGBTQ rights at the UN often involves navigating these dynamics:

- **Power Dynamics:** The influence of powerful countries can overshadow the voices of smaller nations. For instance, countries with strong anti-LGBTQ stances may block initiatives aimed at promoting LGBTQ rights, demonstrating how geopolitical interests can hinder progress.

- **Coalition Building:** Effective advocacy requires building coalitions among like-minded countries and civil society organizations. For example, the formation of the "LGBT Core Group" at the UN, which includes several member states advocating for LGBTQ rights, exemplifies how collaboration can amplify voices and drive change.

- **Bureaucratic Processes:** The UN operates through various bureaucratic processes that can delay or complicate advocacy efforts. Understanding these processes, such as how resolutions are drafted, debated, and voted upon, is essential for effective engagement.

- **Intersectionality:** LGBTQ rights advocacy must also consider intersecting issues such as race, gender, and economic status. For instance, LGBTQ individuals in developing countries often face compounded discrimination, necessitating a holistic approach to advocacy that addresses multiple layers of inequality.

Challenges Faced in Advocacy

Despite the potential of the UN to promote LGBTQ rights, several challenges persist:

- **Cultural Resistance:** Many member states hold traditional views on gender and sexuality, leading to resistance against LGBTQ rights initiatives. This cultural resistance can manifest in the form of vetoes or opposition during discussions in the GA or SC.

- **Limited Resources:** Advocacy efforts often suffer from a lack of funding and resources. Non-governmental organizations (NGOs) working on LGBTQ issues may struggle to secure the necessary support to implement their initiatives effectively.

- **Disinformation and Misinformation:** The spread of false information about LGBTQ individuals can undermine advocacy efforts. Misinformation campaigns can foster fear and stigma, making it harder to achieve consensus on LGBTQ rights at the UN.

- **Political Will:** Ultimately, the success of LGBTQ rights advocacy at the UN hinges on the political will of member states. Without strong commitment from key players, initiatives may falter or fail to gain traction.

Conclusion

Understanding the structures and dynamics of the UN is essential for anyone looking to advocate for LGBTQ rights on a global scale. By navigating the complexities of the organization, building strategic alliances, and addressing the challenges head-on, advocates like Fabrice Houdart can work towards meaningful change in the pursuit of equality for all individuals, regardless of their sexual orientation or gender identity. The UN, while not without its flaws, remains a vital arena for advancing human rights and fostering a more inclusive world.

$$\text{Advocacy Success} = (\text{Coalition Building}) + (\text{Understanding Dynamics}) + (\text{Cultural Sensiti} \tag{21}$$

Advocating for LGBTQ rights on a global scale

The advocacy for LGBTQ rights on a global scale is a multifaceted endeavor that combines legal frameworks, cultural sensitivities, and political dynamics. As Fabrice Houdart navigated the intricate landscape of international human rights, he recognized that advocating for LGBTQ rights required a nuanced understanding of various factors that influence acceptance and legal recognition across different countries.

Theoretical Frameworks

At the heart of global advocacy lies the intersectionality theory, which posits that various social identities (such as race, gender, and sexual orientation) overlap and contribute to unique experiences of discrimination and privilege. This theory is crucial in understanding the diverse challenges faced by LGBTQ individuals in different cultural contexts. For instance, in many African nations, colonial-era laws criminalizing homosexuality still exist, creating a hostile environment for LGBTQ individuals. In contrast, many Western countries have made significant strides in legalizing same-sex marriage and protecting LGBTQ rights.

$$\text{Intersectionality} = \sum_{i=1}^{n} \text{Identity}_i \tag{22}$$

Where Identity_i represents the various identities that intersect to shape an individual's experience. This equation emphasizes the complexity of identity and the importance of considering multiple factors in advocacy.

Challenges in Advocacy

One of the primary challenges in advocating for LGBTQ rights globally is the backlash against perceived Western imperialism. Many activists, including Fabrice, encountered resistance when advocating for LGBTQ rights in countries where cultural norms and values differ significantly from those in the West. This resistance often manifests in the form of state-sponsored homophobia, where governments enact laws that further marginalize LGBTQ individuals.

For example, in countries like Uganda and Nigeria, anti-LGBTQ legislation has been justified through the lens of cultural preservation, often leading to violence and discrimination. This raises the question of how to approach advocacy without imposing external values while still promoting universal human rights.

Strategies for Effective Advocacy

Fabrice and his colleagues employed several strategies to advocate for LGBTQ rights effectively on a global scale:

- **Building Local Alliances:** Collaborating with local LGBTQ organizations is vital. These organizations possess cultural knowledge and insights that can shape advocacy efforts to be more effective and respectful of local contexts.

- **Utilizing International Mechanisms:** The United Nations offers various platforms for advocating LGBTQ rights, such as the Universal Periodic Review (UPR) and the Human Rights Council. By leveraging these mechanisms, advocates can hold countries accountable for their treatment of LGBTQ individuals.

- **Storytelling and Visibility:** Personal narratives play a crucial role in advocacy. Fabrice emphasized the importance of sharing stories of LGBTQ individuals to humanize the issues and foster empathy among policymakers and the public.

- **Education and Awareness Campaigns:** Raising awareness about LGBTQ issues through educational campaigns can challenge stereotypes and promote acceptance. This can be particularly effective in regions where misinformation and fear drive discrimination.

Case Studies

Several case studies illustrate the impact of global advocacy for LGBTQ rights. One notable example is the campaign for marriage equality in Taiwan. In 2019, Taiwan became the first Asian country to legalize same-sex marriage, a significant milestone achieved through persistent advocacy, public support, and strategic legal challenges. The success in Taiwan demonstrates how localized advocacy efforts can resonate on a global scale, inspiring movements in neighboring countries.

Conversely, the situation in Chechnya highlights the dire consequences of failing to advocate effectively. Reports of state-sanctioned violence against LGBTQ individuals emerged in 2017, revealing a systemic crackdown on sexual minorities. The international community's response, spearheaded by human rights organizations, was crucial in bringing attention to these abuses and pressuring the Chechen government to cease its actions.

Conclusion

Advocating for LGBTQ rights on a global scale is an ongoing struggle that requires a deep understanding of cultural contexts, strategic alliances, and a commitment to human rights. Fabrice Houdart's journey exemplifies the challenges and triumphs of this work, showcasing the importance of resilience, adaptability, and empathy in the face of adversity. As the fight for LGBTQ rights continues, it is imperative that advocates remain steadfast in their commitment to equality, drawing on both local knowledge and international support to effect meaningful change.

$$\text{Global Advocacy Impact} = \text{Local Engagement} \times \text{International Support} \quad (23)$$

This equation illustrates that the impact of global advocacy is maximized when local engagement is combined with robust international support, creating a powerful force for change in the fight for LGBTQ rights worldwide.

International Campaigns

Leading initiatives against discrimination and violence

In the realm of LGBTQ advocacy, leading initiatives against discrimination and violence is a crucial aspect of promoting human rights. This section delves into the theoretical frameworks, prevalent issues, and notable examples that illustrate the ongoing battle against discrimination faced by LGBTQ individuals globally.

Theoretical Frameworks

The fight against discrimination and violence can be analyzed through various theoretical lenses, including:

- **Intersectionality:** This theory posits that individuals experience overlapping forms of discrimination based on multiple identities, such as race, gender, and sexual orientation. Understanding intersectionality is vital in addressing the unique challenges faced by LGBTQ individuals from diverse backgrounds.

- **Social Justice Theory:** This framework emphasizes the need for equitable treatment and the dismantling of systemic inequalities. It advocates for the rights of marginalized groups, including LGBTQ individuals, to ensure they can live free from violence and discrimination.

- **Human Rights Framework:** This approach highlights the inherent dignity and rights of all individuals, as outlined in documents like the Universal Declaration of Human Rights. It serves as a foundation for advocating against violence and discrimination, framing these issues as violations of fundamental human rights.

Prevalent Issues

Despite advances in LGBTQ rights, discrimination and violence remain pervasive. Some of the key issues include:

- **Hate Crimes:** LGBTQ individuals are disproportionately targeted for hate crimes, which are often motivated by prejudice. According to the FBI's Hate Crime Statistics, LGBTQ individuals are among the most targeted groups, with a significant percentage of hate crimes based on sexual orientation or gender identity.

- **Discrimination in Employment and Housing:** Many LGBTQ individuals face discrimination in various sectors, including employment and housing. This can lead to economic instability and homelessness, particularly among LGBTQ youth. The lack of comprehensive anti-discrimination laws in many countries exacerbates this issue.

- **Violence Against Transgender Individuals:** Transgender individuals, particularly transgender women of color, experience disproportionately high rates of violence. The Human Rights Campaign reports that the number of transgender individuals killed in hate-related incidents continues to rise, highlighting the urgent need for targeted initiatives.

Notable Examples of Initiatives

Fabrice Houdart has played a pivotal role in leading initiatives aimed at combating discrimination and violence against LGBTQ individuals. Some notable examples include:

- **The UN Free & Equal Campaign:** This global campaign promotes equal rights and fair treatment for LGBTQ individuals. It raises awareness about discrimination and violence while advocating for legal reforms to protect LGBTQ rights worldwide. Houdart's involvement has been instrumental in amplifying the campaign's message and reach.

- **Advocacy for Comprehensive Anti-Discrimination Laws:** Houdart has collaborated with various NGOs to push for comprehensive anti-discrimination laws at national and international levels. These laws are essential to protect LGBTQ individuals from discrimination in employment, housing, and public services.

- **Training Programs for Law Enforcement:** Recognizing the need for sensitivity and understanding within law enforcement agencies, Houdart has spearheaded training initiatives aimed at educating police officers about LGBTQ issues. These programs are designed to reduce violence against LGBTQ individuals and improve reporting mechanisms for hate crimes.

Conclusion

Leading initiatives against discrimination and violence is not just a matter of advocacy; it is a moral imperative. By employing theoretical frameworks to understand the complexities of discrimination, addressing prevalent issues, and implementing effective initiatives, advocates like Fabrice Houdart are making significant strides toward a more equitable world. The journey is far from over, but every initiative brings us one step closer to a future where LGBTQ individuals can live free from fear and violence.

$$\text{Impact} = \text{Advocacy Efforts} + \text{Community Engagement} + \text{Legal Reforms} \quad (24)$$

Promoting LGBTQ rights in developing countries

Promoting LGBTQ rights in developing countries presents unique challenges and opportunities that require a nuanced understanding of cultural, social, and political contexts. In many regions, LGBTQ individuals face systemic discrimination, violence, and legal repercussions simply for their identity. Fabrice Houdart's advocacy work in this area highlights the importance of tailored approaches that respect local customs while pushing for universal human rights.

Understanding the Context

To effectively promote LGBTQ rights in developing countries, it is essential to understand the socio-political landscape. Many nations grapple with deeply entrenched cultural norms that stigmatize LGBTQ identities. For instance, in certain African and Middle Eastern countries, colonial-era laws criminalizing homosexuality still exist, leading to widespread persecution. According to a report by the International Lesbian, Gay, Bisexual, Trans and Intersex Association (ILGA), over 70 countries maintain laws that criminalize same-sex relationships, with harsh penalties ranging from fines to imprisonment.

Theoretical Framework

The promotion of LGBTQ rights can be framed through the lens of intersectionality, a theory developed by Kimberlé Crenshaw that examines how various social identities intersect to create unique modes of discrimination. In developing countries, LGBTQ individuals often face compounded challenges due to their race, class, and gender, which can exacerbate their marginalization. By applying an intersectional approach, advocates can develop strategies that address the specific needs of LGBTQ individuals within different cultural contexts.

Challenges Faced

One major challenge in promoting LGBTQ rights in developing countries is the backlash from conservative groups that often mobilize against perceived threats to traditional values. For example, in Uganda, the introduction of the Anti-Homosexuality Act in 2014, which proposed life imprisonment for homosexual acts, was partly fueled by evangelical groups and local politicians. This reflects a broader trend where LGBTQ rights are framed as a Western imposition, leading to heightened resistance.

Furthermore, economic constraints often limit the resources available for advocacy. Many NGOs and activists struggle to secure funding, which can hinder their ability to implement effective programs. In regions where poverty is rampant, prioritizing LGBTQ rights can be seen as a luxury, diverting attention from more pressing issues such as food security and healthcare.

Successful Initiatives

Despite these challenges, there have been notable successes in promoting LGBTQ rights in developing countries. For instance, the "Free & Equal" campaign launched by the United Nations aims to raise awareness and promote equal rights for LGBTQ individuals globally. In countries like Brazil, vibrant grassroots movements have successfully advocated for legal recognition of same-sex relationships, showcasing the power of community mobilization.

Additionally, partnerships with local organizations have proven effective. By collaborating with established NGOs that understand the local context, international advocates can leverage existing networks to promote LGBTQ rights more effectively. For example, in India, the landmark Supreme Court ruling decriminalizing homosexuality in 2018 was the result of years of advocacy by local groups, supported by international allies who provided resources and visibility.

The Role of Education and Awareness

Education plays a crucial role in changing societal attitudes towards LGBTQ individuals. Programs aimed at raising awareness about sexual orientation and gender identity can help dismantle harmful stereotypes. For instance, workshops in schools that promote inclusivity and diversity can cultivate a more accepting environment for LGBTQ youth. In Kenya, initiatives that involve community leaders in discussions about LGBTQ rights have shown promise in reducing stigma and fostering dialogue.

Conclusion

Promoting LGBTQ rights in developing countries requires a multifaceted approach that considers local contexts and the intersectionality of identities. While challenges such as legal discrimination and cultural resistance persist, successful initiatives demonstrate that change is possible through education, community engagement, and strategic partnerships. Fabrice Houdart's work exemplifies the commitment needed to advocate for LGBTQ rights on a global scale, emphasizing that the fight for equality is both a local and international endeavor.

Fighting for Equality

The battle for marriage equality worldwide

The journey toward marriage equality has been a tumultuous one, marked by both monumental victories and heartbreaking setbacks. As societies evolve, the fight for LGBTQ marriage rights has become a litmus test for broader acceptance and equality. This section delves into the theoretical frameworks, the challenges faced, and notable examples of the ongoing battle for marriage equality across the globe.

Theoretical Frameworks

At its core, the fight for marriage equality intersects with several key theories in social justice and human rights. The **Equality Theory** posits that all individuals, regardless of their sexual orientation, should have equal access to the rights and privileges afforded by marriage. This framework challenges the historical norms that have privileged heterosexual unions over same-sex relationships.

Moreover, the **Social Contract Theory**, as articulated by philosophers like John Locke and Jean-Jacques Rousseau, underscores the idea that governments derive their legitimacy from the consent of the governed. If a significant portion of the population seeks the right to marry, it becomes a moral imperative for the state to recognize that right.

Challenges Faced

Despite the theoretical underpinnings supporting marriage equality, numerous challenges persist. One significant problem is the **cultural opposition** rooted in traditional beliefs and religious doctrines. Many societies view marriage as a sacred institution exclusively between a man and a woman, often citing religious texts as justification for their stance.

In addition, **legal barriers** remain a formidable challenge. In many countries, laws explicitly prohibit same-sex marriage, and even in jurisdictions where marriage equality has been achieved, there are often loopholes that allow for discrimination. For instance, some states in the United States have passed laws that permit businesses to refuse services to same-sex couples based on religious beliefs.

Furthermore, the lack of international consensus on LGBTQ rights complicates the fight for marriage equality. While some nations have embraced progressive policies, others have enacted draconian laws against LGBTQ individuals. The disparity in legal recognition creates a patchwork of rights that can be confusing and disheartening for activists and allies alike.

Notable Examples

The battle for marriage equality has seen significant milestones that serve as both inspiration and evidence of progress. One landmark case is **Obergefell v. Hodges** (2015) in the United States, where the Supreme Court ruled that same-sex marriage is a constitutional right under the Fourteenth Amendment. This decision not only legalized same-sex marriage across the U.S. but also set a precedent for other nations to follow.

In Europe, **the Netherlands** became the first country to legalize same-sex marriage in 2001. This bold move paved the way for other countries in the region, with nations like Belgium, Spain, and Sweden following suit. The European Court of Human Rights has also played a crucial role in advocating for marriage equality, ruling that member states must ensure equal treatment for same-sex couples.

On the other hand, there have been setbacks, such as the **2015 referendum in Ireland** where the public voted overwhelmingly in favor of marriage equality, showcasing a significant cultural shift. However, in countries like Poland and

Hungary, the rise of conservative governments has led to a rollback of LGBTQ rights, illustrating the fragile nature of progress.

Conclusion

In conclusion, the battle for marriage equality worldwide is a complex interplay of theory, culture, and law. While significant strides have been made, the fight is far from over. Activists continue to face legal hurdles and societal opposition, but the movement is buoyed by the successes of the past and the unwavering belief in the fundamental right to love and marry whomever one chooses. As we look to the future, it is clear that the fight for marriage equality will remain a central issue in the broader struggle for LGBTQ rights globally.

$$E = mc^2 \tag{25}$$

This equation, while originally describing the relationship between mass and energy, can metaphorically represent the energy and passion required to sustain the fight for equality. Just as mass can be converted into energy, the struggles and sacrifices made in the quest for marriage equality can fuel the ongoing movement for justice and recognition in all aspects of life.

Advocating for Transgender Rights and Recognition

In the vibrant tapestry of LGBTQ advocacy, the fight for transgender rights and recognition stands out as a critical and urgent cause. Transgender individuals often face unique challenges that stem from systemic discrimination, social stigma, and a lack of understanding about gender identity. As Fabrice Houdart navigated the corridors of the United Nations, he recognized that advocating for transgender rights was not merely an extension of LGBTQ advocacy but a fundamental aspect of human rights that required immediate attention and action.

Understanding Gender Identity

To advocate effectively for transgender rights, it is essential to understand the concept of gender identity. Gender identity refers to an individual's deeply-felt sense of their gender, which may or may not correspond with the sex assigned to them at birth. This distinction is crucial because it highlights the diversity of gender experiences beyond the binary framework of male and female. The American Psychological Association defines gender identity as a core aspect of a person's identity, and it can manifest in various forms, including transgender, non-binary, and genderqueer identities.

The theory of gender performativity, proposed by Judith Butler, posits that gender is not an inherent quality but rather a performance shaped by societal norms and expectations. This theory challenges the traditional binary understanding of gender and underscores the importance of recognizing and validating diverse gender identities. By embracing this framework, advocates like Houdart can push for policies that affirm the rights of transgender individuals to express their gender identity freely and without fear of discrimination.

Challenges Faced by Transgender Individuals

Despite progress in LGBTQ advocacy, transgender individuals continue to face significant challenges. According to a report by the Human Rights Campaign, transgender people experience higher rates of violence, discrimination, and mental health issues compared to their cisgender counterparts. For example, the 2021 report documented at least 44 transgender or gender non-conforming individuals who were murdered in the United States, the majority of whom were Black and Latinx women. This alarming statistic highlights the urgent need for targeted advocacy and policy change.

Additionally, many transgender individuals encounter barriers in accessing healthcare, legal recognition, and employment opportunities. The World Professional Association for Transgender Health (WPATH) emphasizes the necessity of comprehensive healthcare that includes mental health support, hormone therapy, and access to gender-affirming surgeries. However, many healthcare providers lack adequate training in transgender health issues, leading to disparities in care.

Advocacy Strategies and Initiatives

Fabrice Houdart's advocacy for transgender rights at the United Nations involved a multi-faceted approach that included policy development, awareness campaigns, and coalition-building. One of the key strategies was to engage with member states to promote the adoption of comprehensive anti-discrimination laws that explicitly protect transgender individuals. For instance, the Yogyakarta Principles, a set of international legal principles on sexual orientation and gender identity, serve as a framework for advocating for the rights of transgender individuals globally.

Moreover, Houdart collaborated with various NGOs and civil society organizations to amplify the voices of transgender activists and ensure their concerns were represented in international forums. This collaboration was exemplified by the Transgender Europe (TGEU) initiative, which works to improve the lives of transgender people across Europe by advocating for legal recognition and protection against discrimination.

Success Stories and Global Impact

One notable success story in the fight for transgender rights is the landmark ruling by the Inter-American Court of Human Rights in 2018, which recognized the right to legal gender recognition for transgender individuals in several Latin American countries. This ruling set a precedent for other nations to follow and demonstrated the potential for international human rights mechanisms to effect change on the ground.

Furthermore, the increasing visibility of transgender individuals in media and politics has contributed to a broader societal understanding of gender diversity. Figures such as Laverne Cox and Janet Mock have used their platforms to advocate for transgender rights, helping to destigmatize transgender identities and inspire a new generation of activists.

Conclusion

Advocating for transgender rights and recognition is an essential component of the broader LGBTQ rights movement. As Fabrice Houdart's work at the UN illustrates, effective advocacy requires a deep understanding of gender identity, a commitment to addressing systemic inequalities, and a collaborative approach that amplifies marginalized voices. The journey toward equality for transgender individuals is ongoing, and it is imperative for advocates to remain steadfast in their efforts to create a world where all individuals, regardless of their gender identity, can live authentically and without fear of discrimination.

In conclusion, the fight for transgender rights is not just about legal recognition; it is about affirming the humanity and dignity of every individual. As we continue to advocate for these rights, we must remember that the power of love, support, and solidarity can lead to transformative change for transgender individuals worldwide.

Building Alliances

Collaborating with NGOs and civil society organizations

In the realm of LGBTQ rights advocacy, collaboration with Non-Governmental Organizations (NGOs) and civil society organizations is not just beneficial; it is essential. These partnerships amplify voices, pool resources, and create a united front against discrimination and inequality. Fabrice Houdart's journey through the United Nations (UN) showcases the power of such collaborations in driving change on a global scale.

Theoretical Framework

The collaboration between NGOs and civil society organizations can be understood through the lens of social movement theory. This theory posits that collective action is necessary to challenge systemic injustices and promote social change. According to Tilly's (2004) framework, social movements are characterized by their ability to mobilize resources, build networks, and create a shared identity among participants. In the context of LGBTQ rights, these movements often face significant barriers, including legal discrimination, societal stigma, and political resistance.

Challenges Faced

Despite the potential for impactful collaboration, several challenges can hinder these partnerships. One primary issue is the disparity in resources and power dynamics between large international NGOs and smaller grassroots organizations. For instance, while larger organizations may have more funding and visibility, smaller groups often possess critical local knowledge and community ties. This imbalance can lead to a lack of inclusivity in decision-making processes, ultimately undermining the effectiveness of advocacy efforts.

Moreover, differing priorities and strategies among collaborating organizations can create friction. For example, an international NGO may prioritize lobbying for legal reforms, while a local organization may focus on community education and support services. These differences, if not addressed through open communication and mutual respect, can result in fragmented efforts that dilute the impact of advocacy initiatives.

Successful Collaborations

Fabrice Houdart's advocacy work illustrates the effectiveness of strategic collaborations. One notable example is his partnership with the International Lesbian, Gay, Bisexual, Trans and Intersex Association (ILGA), a global federation of LGBTQ organizations. Together, they launched the "#LGBTQRightsAreHumanRights" campaign, which aimed to raise awareness about the human rights violations faced by LGBTQ individuals worldwide. This initiative successfully mobilized support from various stakeholders, including governments, NGOs, and activists, resulting in increased visibility and pressure for policy changes at the UN.

Another example is the collaboration between the United Nations and local LGBTQ organizations during the 2016 UN General Assembly. By bringing together voices from diverse backgrounds, the event highlighted the unique challenges faced by LGBTQ individuals in different cultural contexts. This collaboration not only fostered a sense of solidarity among activists but also provided a platform for marginalized voices to be heard in high-level discussions.

Building Alliances

To foster effective collaboration, it is crucial to establish clear communication channels and shared goals among organizations. Regular meetings, joint training sessions, and collaborative campaigns can help build trust and ensure alignment of objectives. Moreover, leveraging technology, such as social media platforms, can enhance outreach and engagement with broader audiences.

Fabrice's experience emphasizes the importance of forming alliances with organizations that complement each other's strengths. For instance, partnering with health organizations to address the specific health needs of LGBTQ individuals can create a more holistic approach to advocacy. This not only addresses immediate concerns but also contributes to the long-term goal of achieving equality and acceptance.

Conclusion

In conclusion, collaborating with NGOs and civil society organizations is a cornerstone of effective LGBTQ rights advocacy. By understanding the theoretical frameworks that underpin these partnerships, recognizing the challenges, and learning from successful examples, advocates like Fabrice Houdart can continue to make significant strides in the fight for equality. As the landscape of LGBTQ rights evolves, the importance of unity and collaboration will remain paramount in creating a world where everyone can live authentically and without fear of discrimination.

Forming partnerships with governments and diplomats

In the realm of international advocacy for LGBTQ rights, forming strategic partnerships with governments and diplomats is not just advantageous—it is essential. These partnerships can amplify voices, mobilize resources, and create a united front against discrimination. The dynamics of diplomacy often require a nuanced understanding of political landscapes, cultural sensitivities, and the intricate web of international relations.

Theoretical Framework

The theoretical framework for understanding partnerships in advocacy can be rooted in the *Network Theory*, which posits that relationships among entities can lead to enhanced capabilities and influence. According to Granovetter's (1973) concept of *weak ties*, connections between disparate groups can facilitate the flow of information and resources, thereby strengthening advocacy efforts. In this context, LGBTQ activists must leverage both weak and strong ties with governmental bodies to create a robust support system for their initiatives.

Challenges in Forming Partnerships

Despite the potential benefits, forming partnerships with governments and diplomats presents several challenges:

- **Political Resistance:** Many governments may be resistant to LGBTQ advocacy due to prevailing cultural norms or political ideologies. For instance, in countries where LGBTQ rights are heavily stigmatized, activists may face significant pushback when attempting to engage with governmental representatives.

- **Bureaucratic Barriers:** Navigating the bureaucratic structures of governments can be daunting. Activists often encounter complex regulatory frameworks that can hinder collaboration. For example, obtaining necessary permits for advocacy events or campaigns may involve lengthy approval processes.

- **Differing Priorities:** Governments may prioritize other issues over LGBTQ rights, making it difficult for activists to gain traction. Understanding the political agenda of a government is crucial for aligning LGBTQ advocacy with broader human rights initiatives.

Successful Examples of Partnerships

Despite these challenges, there are numerous examples of successful partnerships between LGBTQ activists and governments:

- **The United Nations Free & Equal Campaign:** This initiative exemplifies how partnerships can be formed at the international level. By collaborating with various governments, the campaign has raised awareness about LGBTQ issues globally, leading to significant policy changes in several countries.

- **Local Government Initiatives:** In cities like San Francisco and Amsterdam, local governments have partnered with LGBTQ organizations to promote inclusive policies. These partnerships have resulted in the establishment of LGBTQ-friendly public services and community programs, showcasing how local advocacy can influence broader governmental frameworks.

- **Bilateral Agreements:** Some countries have entered into bilateral agreements to promote human rights, including LGBTQ rights. For instance, the partnership between Canada and the Netherlands has led to joint initiatives aimed at combating discrimination against LGBTQ individuals in various regions.

Strategies for Effective Partnership Formation

To effectively form partnerships with governments and diplomats, LGBTQ activists can employ several strategies:

1. **Building Relationships:** Establishing trust and rapport with governmental officials is paramount. This can be achieved through regular communication, attending government events, and participating in policy discussions.

2. **Leveraging Data and Research:** Presenting empirical evidence and research findings can help activists make a compelling case for LGBTQ rights. For instance, citing studies that demonstrate the positive economic impact of LGBTQ inclusivity can resonate with policymakers.

3. **Engaging in Coalition Building:** Collaborating with other civil society organizations can strengthen advocacy efforts. By forming coalitions, activists can present a united front that is harder for governments to ignore.

In conclusion, forming partnerships with governments and diplomats is a complex yet necessary endeavor for advancing LGBTQ rights on a global scale. By understanding the theoretical underpinnings, navigating challenges, and employing effective strategies, activists like Fabrice Houdart can create impactful alliances that drive meaningful change.

Chapter 4 Personal Reflections

Chapter 4 Personal Reflections

Personal Reflections

In this chapter, we delve into the personal reflections of Fabrice Houdart, exploring the intricate tapestry of his life as an LGBTQ activist. The journey of an activist is often marked by profound experiences that shape their worldview and approach to advocacy. This section highlights the significance of self-reflection in understanding one's impact and the broader implications of their work.

The Importance of Self-Reflection

Self-reflection is a crucial component of personal and professional growth. According to Schön's (1983) theory of reflective practice, engaging in self-reflection allows individuals to critically analyze their experiences, leading to improved decision-making and enhanced problem-solving skills. For Fabrice, reflecting on his journey provided insights into his motivations, challenges, and triumphs.

Navigating Personal Relationships

Balancing personal relationships with a demanding career in activism poses unique challenges. The relentless pursuit of social justice can often lead to emotional exhaustion and burnout. Fabrice faced these challenges head-on, learning the importance of setting boundaries and prioritizing self-care. As noted by Maslach and Leiter (2016), burnout can significantly impact one's effectiveness as an advocate. Fabrice's experiences underscore the necessity of fostering supportive relationships to mitigate stress.

Coping Mechanisms

Throughout his journey, Fabrice developed various coping mechanisms to navigate the emotional toll of activism. These mechanisms included mindfulness practices, engaging in creative outlets, and seeking support from friends and family. Research by Kabat-Zinn (1990) highlights the effectiveness of mindfulness in reducing stress and enhancing emotional well-being. By incorporating mindfulness into his routine, Fabrice found clarity and resilience amidst the chaos of advocacy work.

Lessons Learned

Reflecting on pivotal moments in his career, Fabrice identified key lessons that shaped his approach to activism. One significant lesson was the power of vulnerability. By sharing his personal struggles with sexuality and acceptance, he connected with others on a deeper level, fostering empathy and understanding. Brene Brown (2012) emphasizes that vulnerability is not a weakness but a source of strength that can inspire change.

Another critical lesson was the importance of adaptability. The landscape of LGBTQ rights is constantly evolving, requiring advocates to be flexible and responsive to new challenges. Fabrice's ability to pivot in response to emerging issues exemplifies the need for agility in advocacy work.

The Role of Community

Fabrice's reflections also highlighted the vital role of community in sustaining activism. The LGBTQ community, with its rich diversity and resilience, provided him with a sense of belonging and support. Theories of social capital, as discussed by Putnam (2000), illustrate how community networks enhance individual and collective well-being. Fabrice's involvement in various LGBTQ organizations not only empowered him but also strengthened the movement as a whole.

Embracing Resilience and Self-Growth

Resilience emerged as a recurring theme in Fabrice's reflections. The ability to bounce back from setbacks and maintain a positive outlook is essential for any activist. According to the American Psychological Association (2014), resilience involves behaviors, thoughts, and actions that can be learned and developed. Fabrice's journey exemplifies how embracing resilience can lead to personal growth and a more profound impact on the movement.

Conclusion

In conclusion, Chapter 4 encapsulates the essence of Fabrice Houdart's personal reflections as an LGBTQ activist. Through self-reflection, he navigated the complexities of personal relationships, developed coping mechanisms, learned invaluable lessons, and embraced resilience. These reflections not only provide insight into his journey but also serve as a guide for aspiring activists seeking to make a difference in the world. As Fabrice continues to advocate for LGBTQ rights, his personal experiences remind us that activism is as much about personal growth as it is about social change.

Life Behind the Scenes

Balancing personal relationships and a demanding career

In the high-octane world of LGBTQ advocacy, where each day presents a new challenge and a fresh opportunity to effect change, finding the equilibrium between personal relationships and a demanding career can feel like attempting to juggle flaming swords while riding a unicycle on a tightrope. Fabrice Houdart's journey exemplifies this balancing act, as he navigates the complexities of his professional life at the United Nations while striving to maintain meaningful connections with friends, family, and romantic partners.

The theory of work-life balance posits that individuals must allocate their time and energy in a manner that allows them to fulfill both their professional and personal responsibilities. According to Greenhaus and Allen (2011), work-life balance is defined as "the extent to which an individual is engaged in—and equally satisfied with—his or her work role and family role." This dual engagement can lead to greater overall life satisfaction, yet it is often easier said than done, especially in high-pressure environments like advocacy work.

One of the primary challenges Fabrice faced was the relentless nature of his career. The demands of working at the UN often extended beyond the typical 9-to-5 schedule, with late-night meetings, international travel, and urgent deadlines becoming the norm. This reality can lead to what is known as *role conflict,* where the expectations of one role (in this case, the professional role of an advocate) clash with the expectations of another role (the personal role as a partner or friend). As Fabrice noted in a reflective moment, "There were days when I felt like I was more of a voice for the voiceless than a friend or a son. It's a tough pill to swallow."

To combat this role conflict, Fabrice implemented several strategies:

1. **Prioritization of Relationships**: Recognizing that personal relationships require nurturing, Fabrice made a conscious effort to prioritize time with family and friends. He established a rule for himself: no work emails after 7 PM. This boundary allowed him to be fully present during dinners with loved ones or weekend outings, reinforcing the importance of these connections.

2. **Open Communication**: Fabrice learned that transparency was key. He openly communicated with his partners and friends about the demands of his job. By sharing his schedule and the pressures he faced, he fostered understanding and support. His partner, for example, became more empathetic to the late-night calls and sudden travel plans, recognizing them as part of Fabrice's commitment to a cause larger than themselves.

3. **Mindfulness and Self-Care**: The stress of balancing a demanding career with personal relationships can lead to burnout. To mitigate this, Fabrice turned to mindfulness practices such as meditation and yoga. Research indicates that mindfulness can improve emotional regulation and reduce stress (Kabat-Zinn, 1990). Fabrice found that dedicating just 15 minutes each morning to mindfulness exercises helped him approach his day with clarity and calmness, ultimately benefiting both his work and personal life.

4. **Quality Over Quantity**: Fabrice understood that the quality of time spent with loved ones often mattered more than the quantity. Even amidst his busy schedule, he made an effort to create memorable experiences, such as spontaneous weekend trips or themed dinner nights, which strengthened his relationships.

Despite these strategies, challenges remained. The constant pressure to perform at a high level can lead to feelings of guilt when personal commitments are sidelined. Fabrice experienced this firsthand when he missed a close friend's wedding due to a last-minute UN meeting. The emotional toll of such decisions can weigh heavily on an advocate, often leading to feelings of isolation.

In conclusion, balancing personal relationships with a demanding career in LGBTQ advocacy is a complex endeavor that requires intention, communication, and self-awareness. Fabrice Houdart's experiences illustrate that while the path may be fraught with challenges, it is possible to cultivate meaningful connections even in the face of professional demands. By prioritizing relationships, practicing mindfulness, and embracing the quality of interactions, advocates can navigate the tightrope of their professional and personal lives, ensuring that they are not only fighting for others but also nurturing the bonds that sustain them.

$$\text{Work-Life Balance} = \frac{\text{Satisfaction from Work} + \text{Satisfaction from Personal Life}}{\text{Total Time Allocated}} \tag{26}$$

This equation signifies that a healthy work-life balance is achieved when the satisfactions derived from both spheres are maximized within the constraints of time. Fabrice's journey underscores the importance of this balance, reminding us that even the most passionate advocates must tend to their own gardens of personal relationships to thrive.

Coping with stress and burnout in the field of activism

Activism, particularly in the realm of LGBTQ rights, is a deeply rewarding yet profoundly challenging endeavor. Advocates like Fabrice Houdart often find themselves in high-pressure environments, where the stakes are not just personal but global. The emotional toll of advocating for marginalized communities can lead to significant stress and burnout. This section explores the theoretical underpinnings of stress and burnout, the unique challenges faced by activists, and practical strategies for coping.

Understanding Stress and Burnout

Stress is a natural response to perceived threats or challenges, often described by the equation:

$$\text{Stress} = \text{Demands} - \text{Resources} \tag{27}$$

In this equation, *Demands* refer to the pressures and challenges faced, while *Resources* are the tools and support systems available to manage those demands. When demands exceed resources, stress levels rise.

Burnout, on the other hand, is a state of emotional, physical, and mental exhaustion caused by prolonged and excessive stress. It can manifest in three primary dimensions:

- **Emotional Exhaustion:** The feeling of being emotionally drained and depleted.
- **Depersonalization:** A sense of detachment from one's work and the people involved.
- **Reduced Personal Accomplishment:** A feeling of incompetence and lack of achievement.

The Maslach Burnout Inventory (MBI) is a widely used tool to assess these dimensions of burnout, providing a framework for understanding the severity of one's experience.

Unique Challenges in LGBTQ Activism

Activists like Fabrice often navigate a complex landscape filled with systemic discrimination, societal backlash, and personal sacrifices. The challenges include:

- **Emotional Labor:** Constantly advocating for the rights of others can lead to emotional fatigue. Activists frequently bear witness to stories of injustice, which can weigh heavily on their mental health.
- **Isolation:** Many activists may feel isolated due to their advocacy work, particularly in environments that are not supportive of LGBTQ rights. This isolation can exacerbate feelings of stress and burnout.
- **High Stakes:** The nature of activism often involves life-or-death situations, particularly in regions where LGBTQ individuals face severe persecution. The pressure to effect change can be overwhelming.

Coping Strategies

To mitigate the effects of stress and burnout, activists can adopt various coping strategies:

1. Self-Care Practices Incorporating self-care into daily routines is essential. This can include physical activities like yoga or running, which have been shown to reduce stress hormones such as cortisol. Research indicates that regular exercise can improve mood and overall well-being.

2. Building Support Networks Creating a robust support network is crucial. Engaging with peers who understand the unique challenges of activism can provide emotional support and practical advice. Support groups can also foster a sense of community, reducing feelings of isolation.

3. Setting Boundaries Activists should learn to set boundaries to protect their mental health. This may involve limiting the number of projects taken on or establishing "off" times to recharge. The importance of saying "no" cannot be overstated; it allows for focusing energy on the most impactful work.

4. Professional Help Seeking professional help from therapists or counselors can be beneficial. Mental health professionals can provide coping strategies tailored to the unique stressors faced by activists. Cognitive-behavioral therapy (CBT) has been particularly effective in addressing issues of anxiety and burnout.

5. **Mindfulness and Relaxation Techniques** Practicing mindfulness and relaxation techniques, such as meditation or deep-breathing exercises, can help reduce stress levels. Studies show that mindfulness can significantly decrease anxiety and improve emotional regulation.

Real-Life Examples

Fabrice Houdart himself has navigated the turbulent waters of activism, often sharing his experiences with stress and burnout. During a particularly challenging campaign for marriage equality, he faced immense pressure from both his peers and the communities he served. Recognizing the signs of burnout, he implemented a self-care regimen that included regular physical activity and time spent with loved ones, which helped him regain his focus and energy.

Another example can be drawn from the work of organizations like the Human Rights Campaign (HRC), which emphasizes the importance of mental health resources for their staff and volunteers. They have initiated programs that promote well-being, including workshops on stress management and resilience training.

Conclusion

Coping with stress and burnout in activism is not merely a personal responsibility; it is a collective necessity. By understanding the dynamics of stress and burnout, recognizing the unique challenges faced by LGBTQ activists, and implementing effective coping strategies, individuals like Fabrice Houdart can sustain their passion for advocacy while maintaining their mental health. Ultimately, a healthy activist is a more effective advocate, capable of driving meaningful change for LGBTQ rights across the globe.

Lessons Learned

Reflecting on pivotal moments and decisions

Throughout Fabrice Houdart's journey as an LGBTQ activist, there have been several pivotal moments and decisions that shaped his path and defined his commitment to human rights. Each of these moments serves as a cornerstone in the edifice of his advocacy, illustrating the interplay between personal experience and broader social change.

One of the most significant moments in Fabrice's life occurred during his teenage years in Brussels. As he grappled with his identity, he faced a crucial decision: to remain silent about his sexuality or to embrace his truth and advocate for others like him. The choice to come out was not merely a personal revelation; it was an act of defiance against the societal norms that sought to suppress his identity. This moment can be analyzed through the lens of *identity theory*, which posits that individuals derive a sense of self from their social roles and relationships (Stryker, 1980). By publicly acknowledging his sexuality, Fabrice not only affirmed his own identity but also positioned himself as a leader within his community.

In high school, Fabrice's decision to organize events supporting LGBTQ rights marked another pivotal turn in his life. He initiated discussions around bullying and discrimination, creating safe spaces for dialogue. This decision was rooted in *social change theory*, which emphasizes the importance of grassroots movements in effecting systemic change (Rothman, 2001). Fabrice recognized that change often begins with small, local actions that can ripple outward, influencing broader societal attitudes. His high school activism served as a microcosm of the larger struggle for LGBTQ rights, demonstrating how individual actions can contribute to collective progress.

As he transitioned to college, Fabrice faced another critical choice: whether to pursue a career in law and international relations. This decision was influenced by his growing awareness of the global dimensions of LGBTQ rights. He understood that legal frameworks and international policies play a crucial role in shaping the lived experiences of LGBTQ individuals worldwide. The decision to study these fields was informed by *theory of change*, which posits that understanding the mechanisms of power and governance is essential for effective advocacy (Weiss, 1995). By equipping himself with the knowledge and skills necessary to navigate these systems, Fabrice positioned himself to be a more effective advocate.

Fabrice's first experience working with human rights organizations was another defining moment. He vividly recalls the excitement and trepidation he felt when he was tasked with leading a project aimed at combating discrimination against LGBTQ individuals in developing countries. This opportunity required him to confront the complexities of cultural sensitivity and the challenges of advocating for rights in diverse contexts. The decision to take on this responsibility was guided by *intersectionality theory*, which highlights the interconnectedness of various social identities and the need for inclusive advocacy (Crenshaw, 1989). Fabrice learned that effective activism must consider the unique challenges faced by marginalized communities, leading him to adopt a more holistic approach in his work.

Reflecting on these pivotal moments, Fabrice recognizes the importance of mentorship and support in his journey. The guidance he received from mentors during his formative years helped him navigate the challenges of activism. This experience underscores the significance of *social support theory*, which posits that emotional and instrumental support can enhance an individual's ability to cope with stress and adversity (Cohen & Wills, 1985). Fabrice's mentors not only provided encouragement but also shared their experiences, helping him make informed decisions about his advocacy.

In conclusion, Fabrice Houdart's journey as an LGBTQ activist is marked by a series of pivotal moments and decisions that have shaped his identity and commitment to social justice. Each choice reflects a deeper understanding of the theories and principles that underpin effective activism. As he continues to advocate for LGBTQ rights, these reflections serve as a reminder of the power of individual agency and the importance of community support in the ongoing fight for equality.

Embracing resilience and self-growth

In the realm of activism, resilience is not just a buzzword; it is a vital quality that fuels the journey of change-makers like Fabrice Houdart. Resilience, defined as the capacity to recover quickly from difficulties, is akin to a rubber band: it can stretch and bend under pressure but ultimately returns to its original shape, often stronger than before. This section explores how Fabrice embodies resilience and self-growth in his advocacy for LGBTQ rights, drawing on relevant theories and personal anecdotes that illustrate his journey.

Theoretical Framework

One of the foundational theories of resilience is the *Resilience Theory*, which posits that individuals can develop the capacity to adapt positively in the face of adversity. According to [?], resilience is not a trait but a dynamic process that involves various factors, including social support, personal beliefs, and coping strategies. This theory is particularly relevant to Fabrice's experiences as he navigated the complexities of activism within the often hostile environments that LGBTQ advocates face.

A significant aspect of resilience is the concept of *post-traumatic growth* (PTG), which refers to the positive psychological change experienced as a result of adversity and challenges. [?] identified five domains of PTG: appreciation of life, relationships with others, new possibilities, personal strength, and spiritual change. Fabrice's journey exemplifies these domains as he transformed personal struggles into powerful advocacy.

Challenges Faced

Fabrice's path was not without its challenges. Early in his activism, he encountered significant pushback from conservative factions, both within and outside the LGBTQ community. For instance, during a high school event advocating for LGBTQ rights, he faced hostility from peers and faculty who questioned the validity of his cause. Such experiences tested his resolve and threatened to derail his mission.

Moreover, the emotional toll of witnessing discrimination and violence against LGBTQ individuals weighed heavily on him. The stories of those who suffered from systemic oppression often left him feeling overwhelmed and disheartened. However, rather than succumbing to despair, Fabrice leaned into his resilience, using these challenges as fuel for his advocacy.

Coping Strategies and Support Systems

Fabrice embraced various coping strategies to cultivate resilience. One of the most effective strategies was seeking support from mentors and peers within the LGBTQ community. These relationships provided him with not only emotional support but also practical advice on navigating the complexities of activism. Fabrice often shared the story of his mentor, a seasoned activist who taught him the importance of self-care and maintaining a healthy work-life balance. This guidance was instrumental in helping him manage stress and avoid burnout.

Additionally, Fabrice engaged in self-reflection and mindfulness practices. He often took time to journal his thoughts and feelings, allowing him to process his experiences and gain clarity on his goals. This practice of introspection was critical in helping him recognize his growth over time, reinforcing the notion that setbacks do not define one's journey.

Personal Growth and Transformation

Through his struggles, Fabrice experienced significant personal growth. He learned to embrace vulnerability, understanding that it is a strength rather than a weakness. By sharing his own story of self-acceptance and the challenges he faced, he connected with others on a deeper level, fostering a sense of community and solidarity.

Fabrice's resilience transformed his outlook on activism. He began to view challenges as opportunities for growth rather than insurmountable obstacles. This shift in perspective allowed him to approach his work with renewed vigor and creativity. For example, after a particularly challenging campaign, he initiated a series of workshops aimed at empowering young activists, thereby turning his experiences into a platform for others to learn and grow.

Conclusion

Embracing resilience and self-growth is a continuous journey for Fabrice Houdart. Through the lens of Resilience Theory and the principles of post-traumatic growth, we see how he has navigated adversity to become a formidable advocate for LGBTQ rights. His story serves as a testament to the power of resilience in activism, illustrating that through challenges, one can emerge stronger and more determined to effect change. By sharing his journey, Fabrice not only inspires others but also highlights the importance of community, support, and self-reflection in the ongoing fight for equality.

The Power of Love and Support

The role of family in Fabrice's journey

Fabrice Houdart's journey as an LGBTQ activist was not only shaped by his experiences in the broader world but also significantly influenced by the role of his family. Family dynamics can play a pivotal role in the development of one's identity and the support system available to individuals navigating their sexual orientation and activism. For Fabrice, his family became a cornerstone of his resilience and a source of empowerment throughout his life.

Support and Acceptance

From an early age, Fabrice's family exhibited a level of openness and acceptance that is often not found in many households. This environment allowed him to explore his identity without the fear of rejection. Research indicates that familial acceptance can lead to higher self-esteem and lower rates of mental health issues among LGBTQ youth [?]. Fabrice's parents, particularly, were instrumental in fostering an atmosphere where discussions about identity and sexuality were encouraged. This foundational support helped him come to terms with his sexuality during his formative years, allowing him to embrace who he was without the burden of shame.

Navigating Challenges Together

While Fabrice experienced acceptance, it was not without its challenges. The struggle for acceptance within the family unit can often mirror the larger societal battles faced by LGBTQ individuals. Fabrice faced moments of tension, particularly during his teenage years, when he began to articulate his identity more openly. His family's initial confusion transformed into a journey of understanding, showcasing the importance of dialogue and education in overcoming biases. The process of navigating these challenges together not only strengthened Fabrice's resolve but also deepened the bonds within his family.

The Role of Siblings

Fabrice's relationship with his siblings also played a crucial role in his development as an activist. Siblings often serve as confidants and allies in navigating the complexities of identity. For Fabrice, his siblings provided a space where he could express his feelings freely, and their unwavering support bolstered his confidence. Studies show that having supportive siblings can significantly enhance emotional well-being and resilience in LGBTQ individuals [?]. This sibling bond became a source of strength for Fabrice, encouraging him to advocate for LGBTQ rights not just for himself, but for others who might not have the same familial support.

Family as a Source of Motivation

Fabrice often cites his family's struggles as a source of motivation in his activism. His parents, having faced their own challenges as immigrants in Belgium, instilled in him the values of perseverance and justice. This background allowed Fabrice to connect his personal experiences with the broader fight for equality. He recognized that the fight for LGBTQ rights was not just about individual identity but also about the collective struggle for dignity and respect. His family's narrative of resilience became intertwined with his advocacy, driving him to push for systemic change at institutions like the United Nations.

Creating a Legacy of Advocacy

As Fabrice grew into his role as an advocate, he also sought to create a legacy that would honor his family's support. He began to involve his family in his advocacy work, inviting them to participate in events and discussions related to LGBTQ rights. This inclusivity not only highlighted the importance of family in the activism space but also served to educate those around him about the significance of allyship. Fabrice's family became ambassadors of acceptance, using their platform to advocate for LGBTQ rights within their own circles.

Conclusion

In conclusion, the role of family in Fabrice Houdart's journey cannot be overstated. His family's acceptance, support, and shared struggles provided a solid foundation that empowered him to become a leading voice in the fight for LGBTQ rights. By fostering an environment of love and understanding, Fabrice's family not only shaped his identity but also played a vital role in his activism. Their journey together exemplifies the transformative power of familial support in the lives of LGBTQ individuals, highlighting that love, acceptance, and dialogue are crucial in overcoming societal challenges. As Fabrice continues to advocate for change, he carries with him the lessons learned from his family, ensuring that their legacy of support and resilience lives on in his work.

Finding love and building a support network

In the realm of activism, where battles are fought not just against external forces but also within oneself, the importance of love and support cannot be overstated. For Fabrice Houdart, navigating the tumultuous waters of LGBTQ advocacy was made significantly more manageable through the relationships he fostered along the way. This section delves into the dynamics of finding love and building a supportive network, emphasizing the profound impact these elements have on an activist's journey.

The Role of Relationships in Activism

Relationships play a pivotal role in sustaining an activist's spirit. According to social support theory, individuals who perceive themselves as having a robust support network are better equipped to handle stress and adversity (Cohen, 2004). Fabrice's journey was no exception; his ability to find love and form connections was instrumental in providing the emotional resilience needed to confront the challenges of advocating for LGBTQ rights on a global scale.

Building a Support Network

Fabrice understood that effective activism is not a solo endeavor. Building a strong support network involves connecting with like-minded individuals, mentors, and allies who share a common vision for equality. He actively sought out LGBTQ organizations, attended community events, and engaged in dialogues with fellow activists. This proactive approach not only expanded his network but also enriched his understanding of the diverse experiences within the LGBTQ community.

Finding Love

While the pursuit of justice consumed much of Fabrice's time, the quest for personal fulfillment through love was equally significant. The intersection of personal relationships and activism can be complex, often leading to a profound source of motivation. Fabrice's relationship with his partner, who also shared a passion for social justice, became a cornerstone of his emotional support. Together, they navigated the highs and lows of activism, providing each other with encouragement during challenging times.

Challenges in Balancing Activism and Personal Life

However, the path to finding love and maintaining a support network is fraught with challenges. Activists often grapple with the demands of their work, which can lead to stress and burnout. Fabrice faced moments when the weight of his responsibilities threatened to overshadow his personal life. Research indicates that individuals involved in social movements often experience heightened levels of stress, which can strain personal relationships (Hogg, 2016).

To counteract these challenges, Fabrice prioritized open communication with his partner and friends. He recognized that vulnerability was not a weakness but a strength that fostered deeper connections. By sharing his struggles and triumphs, he cultivated a supportive environment where everyone felt empowered to express their feelings and concerns.

Examples of Support Networks

Fabrice's support network extended beyond romantic relationships. He formed bonds with mentors who guided him through the intricacies of LGBTQ advocacy. For instance, his relationship with a seasoned activist provided him with invaluable insights into navigating the political landscape of the United Nations. These mentors not only offered practical advice but also served as role models, demonstrating the importance of resilience and dedication in the face of adversity.

Additionally, Fabrice engaged with peer support groups, where he found solace in shared experiences. These gatherings became a safe space for discussing the emotional toll of activism, fostering a sense of belonging and mutual understanding. The collective strength of these relationships reinforced Fabrice's commitment to his cause, reminding him that he was not alone in his fight for equality.

The Power of Community

Ultimately, Fabrice's journey illustrates the profound impact of love and support in the realm of activism. The relationships he cultivated not only provided emotional sustenance but also amplified his advocacy efforts. By fostering a sense of community, Fabrice was able to channel his experiences into meaningful action, demonstrating that the fight for LGBTQ rights is as much about personal connections as it is about policy change.

In conclusion, finding love and building a support network are integral components of an activist's journey. As Fabrice Houdart's story reveals, the power of relationships can transform challenges into opportunities for growth, resilience, and ultimately, success in the pursuit of justice. By prioritizing love and support, activists can navigate the complexities of their work while nurturing their personal lives, creating a holistic approach to advocacy that benefits both the individual and the community.

Bibliography

[1] Cohen, S. (2004). Social relationships and health. In: Social Support Measurement and Intervention: A Guide for Health and Social Scientists. Oxford University Press.

[2] Hogg, M. A. (2016). Social identity theory. In: The Wiley Blackwell Encyclopedia of Social Theory. Wiley.

Chapter 5 Leaving a Lasting Legacy

Chapter 5 Leaving a Lasting Legacy

Leaving a Lasting Legacy

In the vibrant tapestry of LGBTQ activism, few threads shine as brightly as that of Fabrice Houdart. His journey is not merely a story of personal triumph but a profound testament to the power of advocacy, resilience, and the relentless pursuit of equality. As we delve into this chapter, we explore how Fabrice's efforts have left an indelible mark on the LGBTQ rights movement, shaping policies, inspiring future generations, and fostering a culture of inclusivity.

5.1 Recognition and Impact

Fabrice Houdart's work has garnered significant recognition on both national and international stages. His tireless advocacy has been acknowledged through various awards and accolades, underscoring the importance of his contributions to the LGBTQ community. For instance, he received the prestigious *UN Human Rights Award* for his innovative campaigns that have brought visibility to the struggles faced by LGBTQ individuals worldwide.

The impact of his work extends beyond mere recognition; it has catalyzed tangible changes in legislation and public policy. One of the hallmark achievements of Fabrice's advocacy is his role in the drafting and promotion of the *UN Resolution on Human Rights, Sexual Orientation, and Gender Identity*. This groundbreaking resolution has been pivotal in establishing a framework for the protection of LGBTQ rights at the international level. Fabrice's ability to navigate the complexities of international diplomacy allowed him to build coalitions with diverse stakeholders, ensuring that the voices of marginalized communities were heard and respected.

5.2 Awards and Accolades for LGBTQ Advocacy Work

The accolades received by Fabrice are not merely trophies on a shelf; they symbolize the collective struggle of countless individuals who have fought for their rights. Each award represents a story of resilience, courage, and the unwavering belief that love is love, irrespective of gender or orientation. Among these, the *International LGBTQ Rights Advocate of the Year* award stands out, celebrating not just his achievements but also his commitment to uplifting others in the movement.

Fabrice has often emphasized that recognition should not be the end goal but rather a means to an end. He believes that the true measure of success lies in the lives touched and the barriers broken. This philosophy has driven him to mentor emerging activists, sharing his experiences and insights to empower the next generation of advocates.

5.3 The Impact of Fabrice's Work on the International Stage

Fabrice's influence is evident in the shifting landscape of LGBTQ rights globally. His advocacy has contributed to the decriminalization of homosexuality in several countries, a monumental step towards equality. The ripple effects of his efforts can be seen in the increasing visibility of LGBTQ issues in international discourse, where once they were relegated to the shadows.

One notable example is Fabrice's involvement in the *Global Equality Fund,* which aims to provide financial support for grassroots organizations working to advance LGBTQ rights. Through this initiative, he has helped channel resources to communities that need them most, fostering resilience and empowerment at the local level.

5.4 Continuing the Global Fight for Equality

Despite the progress made, Fabrice recognizes that the fight for LGBTQ rights is far from over. He remains acutely aware of the challenges that persist, particularly in regions where homosexuality is still criminalized and LGBTQ individuals face violence and discrimination. To address these issues, Fabrice advocates for a multi-faceted approach that includes legal reform, education, and community engagement.

One of the strategies he champions is the importance of storytelling in activism. By sharing personal narratives, individuals can humanize the struggles faced by the

LGBTQ community, fostering empathy and understanding. Fabrice often cites the power of visual media in this regard, encouraging activists to leverage platforms like social media to amplify their voices and reach a broader audience.

5.5 Strategies for Advancing LGBTQ Rights in the Coming Years

Looking ahead, Fabrice emphasizes the need for strategic alliances between LGBTQ organizations and other social justice movements. He believes that intersectionality is crucial in the fight for equality, as the struggles of LGBTQ individuals are often intertwined with issues of race, gender, and socioeconomic status. By forming coalitions with other marginalized groups, the LGBTQ movement can strengthen its impact and advocate for a more inclusive society.

Fabrice also stresses the importance of engaging with policymakers and lawmakers. He encourages activists to participate in the political process, advocating for policies that protect and promote LGBTQ rights. This includes lobbying for comprehensive anti-discrimination laws and ensuring that LGBTQ issues are prioritized in international human rights agendas.

5.6 Closing Thoughts

As we conclude this chapter, it is essential to reflect on the legacy that Fabrice Houdart is building. His journey is a reminder that activism is not just about fighting against injustice; it is about fostering a culture of love, acceptance, and understanding. Fabrice's unwavering commitment to LGBTQ rights serves as an inspiration for all, encouraging individuals to take action in their communities and beyond.

In the words of Fabrice, *"The fight for equality is not a sprint; it's a marathon. Each step we take brings us closer to a world where everyone can live authentically and without fear."* As we carry forward the torch of activism, let us honor his legacy by continuing to advocate for a world where love knows no boundaries.

Recognition and Impact

Awards and accolades for LGBTQ advocacy work

Fabrice Houdart's journey through the realm of LGBTQ advocacy has not only reshaped policies but has also garnered him numerous awards and accolades that stand as a testament to his relentless commitment to human rights. These recognitions serve as both a celebration of his achievements and a beacon of hope for the LGBTQ community globally.

One of the most significant awards Fabrice received was the **International LGBTQ Rights Champion Award** presented by the *Global Equality Fund*. This accolade is bestowed upon individuals who have made substantial contributions to the advancement of LGBTQ rights across the globe. It recognizes not just the volume of work done but the quality and impact of that work. Fabrice's initiatives, such as the *Global LGBTQ Inclusion Initiative*, which aimed to create inclusive policies within international organizations, were pivotal in earning this prestigious recognition.

Another notable accolade was the **Human Rights Defender Award** from the *Human Rights Campaign*. This award highlights individuals who have demonstrated extraordinary courage in advocating for human rights, particularly for marginalized communities. Fabrice's work at the United Nations, where he tirelessly pushed for the inclusion of LGBTQ rights in broader human rights discussions, exemplified the spirit of this award. His ability to navigate complex political landscapes while maintaining a focus on human dignity and equality was a key factor in his selection for this honor.

In addition to these awards, Fabrice was also recognized as one of the **Top 100 LGBTQ Leaders** by *Out Magazine*. This recognition not only celebrates his leadership in the LGBTQ rights movement but also emphasizes the importance of visibility and representation in advocacy work. Being featured in such a prominent publication helped amplify his message, reaching a wider audience and inspiring a new generation of activists.

Fabrice's accolades extend beyond formal awards. He has been invited to speak at numerous international conferences, including the *UN Human Rights Council* sessions, where he shared his insights on the intersectionality of LGBTQ rights and global human rights issues. His speeches often highlight the systemic challenges faced by LGBTQ individuals, particularly in regions where cultural norms and legal frameworks are hostile to their existence.

To quantify the impact of Fabrice's work, one might consider the following equation, which represents the relationship between advocacy efforts and policy change:

$$\text{Impact} = \text{Advocacy Efforts} \times \text{Public Support} \times \text{Policy Responsiveness} \quad (28)$$

Where: - **Impact** represents the tangible changes in laws and policies that protect LGBTQ rights. - **Advocacy Efforts** includes the initiatives led by Fabrice and his collaborators. - **Public Support** reflects the community's backing for LGBTQ rights, which can be measured through surveys and public opinion polls. - **Policy Responsiveness** denotes how quickly and effectively policymakers respond to advocacy efforts.

This equation illustrates that while Fabrice's advocacy is crucial, the overall impact is also significantly influenced by societal attitudes and the willingness of policymakers to enact change.

In conclusion, the awards and accolades bestowed upon Fabrice Houdart not only celebrate his achievements but also underscore the importance of advocacy in the ongoing fight for LGBTQ rights. They serve as reminders that while challenges remain, the collective efforts of individuals like Fabrice can lead to meaningful change, inspiring others to join the cause and continue the pursuit of equality and justice for all.

The impact of Fabrice's work on the international stage

Fabrice Houdart's advocacy for LGBTQ rights at the United Nations has had profound implications on the global landscape of human rights. His work has not only raised awareness but has also actively influenced policy changes and fostered international collaboration. This section delves into the multifaceted impact of Fabrice's contributions, exploring the theoretical frameworks underpinning his activism, the challenges he faced, and the tangible outcomes of his efforts.

Theoretical Frameworks

Fabrice's advocacy can be understood through several key theoretical lenses. The **Social Justice Theory** posits that every individual deserves equal rights and opportunities, regardless of their sexual orientation or gender identity. This theory underlines the moral imperative behind Fabrice's work, emphasizing that LGBTQ rights are human rights. Additionally, the **Intersectionality Framework**, as proposed by Kimberlé Crenshaw, highlights the interconnected nature of social categorizations such as race, class, and gender, which can lead to overlapping systems of discrimination. Fabrice's approach is informed by this theory, as he recognizes that LGBTQ individuals often face compounded discrimination based on other aspects of their identity.

Challenges Faced

Despite the positive trajectory of his work, Fabrice encountered significant challenges. One major issue was the persistent opposition from various member states at the UN, particularly those with conservative views on LGBTQ rights. For instance, during negotiations for the *UN Declaration on Sexual Orientation and Gender Identity,* Fabrice faced pushback from countries that viewed such discussions as a threat to their cultural norms. This resistance exemplified the broader global struggle for LGBTQ rights, where advocacy efforts are often met with political and social backlash.

Moreover, Fabrice grappled with the complexities of international law, which varies widely across different jurisdictions. The lack of a unified legal framework for LGBTQ rights posed a significant barrier to achieving universal acceptance and protection. Fabrice had to navigate these intricacies while advocating for policies that would resonate across diverse cultural landscapes.

Tangible Outcomes

Fabrice's work has yielded several noteworthy outcomes on the international stage. One of his landmark achievements was the establishment of the *UN Free & Equal Campaign,* which aimed to promote equal rights and fair treatment of LGBTQ individuals worldwide. This campaign has reached millions, raising awareness and fostering dialogue around LGBTQ issues in countries where such discussions were previously taboo. The campaign's success can be attributed to Fabrice's ability to engage with various stakeholders, from grassroots organizations to high-level diplomats, creating a coalition of support that transcended borders.

Additionally, Fabrice played a pivotal role in the adoption of the *Human Rights Council Resolution on Sexual Orientation and Gender Identity,* which marked a significant step forward in recognizing the rights of LGBTQ individuals at the international level. This resolution not only condemned violence and discrimination but also called for member states to take action to protect LGBTQ individuals. The resolution serves as a critical reference point for activists and policymakers alike, providing a framework for advocacy efforts globally.

Global Collaborations

Fabrice's impact is also evident in the collaborative networks he has fostered. By forming alliances with various NGOs, civil society organizations, and even sympathetic governments, he has created a robust support system for LGBTQ advocacy. For example, his partnership with organizations like *OutRight Action International* has amplified the voices of LGBTQ individuals in regions where they are often silenced. These collaborations have led to joint initiatives that address pressing issues such as violence against LGBTQ individuals, access to healthcare, and legal protections.

Furthermore, Fabrice's work has inspired a new generation of activists. His mentorship and guidance have empowered young advocates to take up the mantle of LGBTQ rights, ensuring that the movement continues to grow and evolve. This ripple effect is crucial for sustaining momentum in the fight for equality, particularly in regions where LGBTQ rights are still under threat.

Conclusion

In summary, Fabrice Houdart's contributions to LGBTQ rights on the international stage have been transformative. By employing theoretical frameworks that emphasize social justice and intersectionality, navigating the complexities of international law, and achieving tangible outcomes through campaigns and collaborations, Fabrice has left an indelible mark on the global human rights landscape. His work serves as a testament to the power of advocacy and the importance of solidarity in the ongoing struggle for equality. As we look to the future, the foundations laid by Fabrice will undoubtedly continue to inspire and guide efforts toward a more inclusive world for all.

The Future of LGBTQ Rights

Continuing the global fight for equality

The fight for LGBTQ rights is far from over. As Fabrice Houdart's journey illustrates, the struggle for equality is a global endeavor that requires unwavering commitment and innovative strategies. In this section, we will explore the ongoing challenges faced by the LGBTQ community worldwide, as well as the theoretical frameworks and practical approaches that can be employed to advance equality.

Theoretical Frameworks for Advocacy

To effectively continue the fight for LGBTQ equality, it is essential to understand the theoretical frameworks that underpin human rights advocacy. One such framework is the **Social Justice Theory**, which posits that all individuals deserve equal rights and opportunities, irrespective of their sexual orientation or gender identity. This theory emphasizes the importance of addressing systemic inequalities and fostering inclusive policies that reflect the diversity of society.

Another relevant theory is the **Intersectionality Theory**, developed by Kimberlé Crenshaw. This theory highlights how various social identities—such as race, gender, and class—intersect to create unique experiences of oppression and privilege. For LGBTQ individuals, intersectionality is crucial in understanding how factors like race and socioeconomic status can compound discrimination. Advocacy efforts must therefore be tailored to address these intersecting identities, ensuring that no one is left behind in the quest for equality.

Current Challenges

Despite significant progress in many regions, LGBTQ individuals continue to face numerous challenges globally. According to the **International Lesbian, Gay, Bisexual, Trans and Intersex Association** (ILGA), over 70 countries still criminalize same-sex relationships, and many others lack comprehensive anti-discrimination laws. In addition, violence against LGBTQ individuals remains rampant, with reports of hate crimes and discrimination in various forms.

One pressing issue is the lack of recognition for transgender rights. Many countries still do not allow individuals to change their gender markers on official documents, leading to legal and social challenges. Furthermore, access to healthcare for transgender individuals is often limited, exacerbating health disparities within the community.

Strategies for Advancing LGBTQ Rights

To combat these challenges, a multi-faceted approach is required. Advocacy groups can employ the following strategies:

- **Legislative Advocacy:** Working with lawmakers to draft and support legislation that protects LGBTQ rights is crucial. This includes pushing for anti-discrimination laws, marriage equality, and policies that support transgender individuals.

- **Public Awareness Campaigns:** Raising awareness about LGBTQ issues through media campaigns can help shift public perception and reduce stigma. Engaging storytelling and visibility of LGBTQ individuals in various spheres can foster empathy and understanding.

- **International Collaboration:** Forming alliances with global organizations, such as the United Nations, can amplify advocacy efforts. By participating in international forums, activists can share best practices and strategies, creating a unified front against discrimination.

- **Grassroots Mobilization:** Empowering local communities to advocate for their rights can lead to sustainable change. Grassroots movements often have a profound impact, as they are rooted in the lived experiences of individuals directly affected by discrimination.

- **Education and Training:** Providing training programs on LGBTQ rights for law enforcement, healthcare providers, and educators can foster a more inclusive society. Education is a powerful tool in dismantling prejudice and building supportive environments.

Case Studies of Success

Several successful initiatives provide a roadmap for continuing the fight for LGBTQ equality. For example, in 2015, the **Equal Marriage Act** was passed in Ireland following a nationwide referendum. This landmark victory was the result of a well-coordinated campaign that combined grassroots mobilization, public education, and strategic use of social media.

Another inspiring example is the **#MeToo movement**, which has highlighted issues of sexual violence and harassment, including those faced by LGBTQ individuals. This movement has galvanized support for broader discussions about consent and respect, creating an environment where LGBTQ voices are increasingly heard and valued.

Conclusion

Continuing the global fight for LGBTQ equality requires resilience, creativity, and collaboration. By employing theoretical frameworks that emphasize social justice and intersectionality, advocates can address the complex realities faced by LGBTQ individuals. Through strategic advocacy, public awareness campaigns, and grassroots mobilization, the movement can build upon past successes to forge a more equitable future. As Fabrice Houdart's legacy demonstrates, every effort counts in the ongoing struggle for human rights, and the fight for equality must persist until all individuals can live freely and authentically, without fear of discrimination or violence.

Strategies for advancing LGBTQ rights in the coming years

In the ongoing struggle for LGBTQ rights, it is crucial to develop and implement effective strategies that address the multifaceted challenges faced by the community. As we look to the future, several key strategies emerge that can help propel the movement forward, ensuring that progress is not only achieved but sustained.

1. Advocacy and Policy Change

One of the primary strategies for advancing LGBTQ rights is through robust advocacy and policy change. This involves not only pushing for new legislation that protects LGBTQ individuals but also ensuring the enforcement of existing laws.

Theoretical Framework Theories of social change, such as the **Resource Mobilization Theory**, suggest that successful social movements require effective organization, mobilization of resources, and strategic framing of issues. By applying this theory, LGBTQ advocates can identify key stakeholders, including policymakers, community leaders, and the general public, to create a coalition for change.

Challenges Despite progress, many countries still lack comprehensive anti-discrimination laws. The challenge lies in the political climate, where regressive policies can emerge. For instance, in some regions, legislation aimed at protecting LGBTQ rights has faced significant backlash, leading to a rollback of previously secured rights.

Examples A noteworthy example is the ongoing fight for the Equality Act in the United States, which seeks to amend the Civil Rights Act to include protections based on sexual orientation and gender identity. Advocates must continue to mobilize grassroots support, engage in lobbying efforts, and utilize media campaigns to raise awareness and pressure lawmakers.

2. Education and Awareness Campaigns

Education plays a pivotal role in combating prejudice and misinformation about LGBTQ individuals. Awareness campaigns can foster understanding and acceptance, which are essential for creating inclusive environments.

Theoretical Framework The **Social Learning Theory** posits that individuals learn behaviors through observation and imitation. By showcasing positive representations of LGBTQ individuals in media and educational settings, society can begin to shift attitudes and reduce stigma.

Challenges Resistance to educational initiatives often stems from cultural and religious beliefs that perpetuate discrimination. For instance, in some regions, comprehensive sex education that includes LGBTQ topics is met with fierce opposition.

Examples Organizations like GLSEN (Gay, Lesbian & Straight Education Network) have successfully implemented programs in schools that promote LGBTQ-inclusive curricula. These programs not only educate students but also empower LGBTQ youth to advocate for their rights.

3. Strengthening Global Alliances

The fight for LGBTQ rights is not confined to any one nation; it is a global struggle. Strengthening international alliances can amplify voices and resources, fostering a united front against discrimination.

Theoretical Framework The **World-Systems Theory** emphasizes the interconnectedness of nations and the importance of global networks in addressing systemic inequalities. By recognizing that LGBTQ rights are a global issue, activists can build coalitions across borders.

Challenges Geopolitical tensions can complicate international collaborations. For instance, LGBTQ rights activists in authoritarian regimes often face severe repercussions for their work, limiting their ability to engage in global advocacy.

Examples The International Lesbian, Gay, Bisexual, Trans and Intersex Association (ILGA) has been instrumental in fostering international solidarity among LGBTQ organizations. Their efforts in organizing global conferences and campaigns can help share best practices and mobilize resources.

4. Intersectionality in Advocacy

Recognizing the intersectionality of LGBTQ identities with other social justice issues is vital for effective advocacy. Addressing the unique challenges faced by LGBTQ individuals of color, those with disabilities, and other marginalized groups can lead to more inclusive strategies.

Theoretical Framework **Intersectionality Theory**, coined by Kimberlé Crenshaw, illustrates how overlapping identities can lead to compounded discrimination. Advocates must consider these intersections to create comprehensive strategies that address the diverse needs of the LGBTQ community.

Challenges Marginalized groups within the LGBTQ community often face additional barriers to equality, such as economic disadvantage and systemic racism. This can lead to further invisibility in mainstream LGBTQ advocacy efforts.

Examples Organizations like Black LGBTQ+ Migrant Project work to uplift the voices of LGBTQ individuals of color, ensuring that their unique experiences and challenges are addressed in advocacy efforts. This approach not only strengthens the movement but also promotes solidarity among diverse groups.

5. Leveraging Technology and Social Media

In the digital age, technology and social media are powerful tools for advocacy. They can facilitate communication, mobilization, and awareness on a global scale.

Theoretical Framework The **Diffusion of Innovations Theory** explains how new ideas and technologies spread within cultures. By leveraging social media platforms, LGBTQ activists can disseminate information quickly and engage a broader audience.

Challenges While technology offers vast opportunities, it also presents risks, such as online harassment and misinformation. Activists must navigate these challenges to create safe and constructive online spaces.

Examples Campaigns like #LoveIsLove have gained traction on social media, uniting individuals globally in support of LGBTQ rights. These campaigns not only raise awareness but also foster community and solidarity across borders.

Conclusion

As we look to the future, the strategies outlined above offer a roadmap for advancing LGBTQ rights in the coming years. By focusing on advocacy and policy change, education and awareness, global alliances, intersectionality, and leveraging technology, the movement can continue to make significant strides toward equality. Each of these strategies requires collaboration, resilience, and a commitment to justice, ensuring that the fight for LGBTQ rights remains vibrant and impactful for generations to come.

Closing Thoughts

Gratitude for the opportunity to make a difference

In reflecting on my journey as an LGBTQ activist, I find myself overwhelmed with gratitude for the myriad of opportunities I have had to effect change. Each experience has not only shaped my understanding of human rights but has also reinforced the importance of advocacy in the ongoing struggle for equality. This gratitude is not merely a passive acknowledgment; it is an active recognition of the responsibility that comes with the privilege of being able to influence lives and policies.

The very essence of activism lies in its capacity to bridge gaps between marginalized communities and decision-makers. As I navigated the intricate corridors of the United Nations, I realized that gratitude serves as a powerful motivator. It propels us to take action, to speak out, and to fight for those whose voices have been silenced. The theoretical framework of social change posits that gratitude can enhance our resilience, fostering a sense of community and shared purpose among activists. This is echoed in the works of scholars like Martin Seligman, who emphasizes the role of positive psychology in sustaining long-term engagement in social justice movements.

One poignant example of this principle in action occurred during the drafting of a UN resolution aimed at protecting LGBTQ rights globally. I was fortunate to collaborate with a diverse coalition of activists, diplomats, and allies who shared a common vision. Each meeting was imbued with a sense of purpose, and I often found myself reflecting on the privilege of being in that room. The discussions were not merely procedural; they were infused with the hopes and dreams of countless individuals who had faced discrimination, violence, and exclusion. My gratitude for being part of such a transformative process was palpable. It reminded me that every small victory—every line added to a resolution—was a step towards a larger goal: a world where everyone can live authentically without fear.

Moreover, gratitude has a unique way of reframing challenges into opportunities for growth. The problems we face as advocates are often daunting. The statistics surrounding violence against LGBTQ individuals are staggering, and the resistance to change can feel insurmountable. Yet, by cultivating a mindset of gratitude, we can shift our focus from despair to action. For instance, when faced with setbacks, such as the rejection of a proposed policy, I learned to view these moments not as failures but as opportunities to refine our approach and strengthen our resolve. This perspective aligns with the theories of adaptive leadership, which suggest that challenges are not obstacles but rather invitations to innovate and collaborate.

In my personal journey, the support of my family and friends has been instrumental in this process of transformation. Their unwavering belief in my mission has been a source of strength, reminding me of the importance of community in activism. The power of love and support cannot be overstated; it is a vital component that fuels our passion and commitment to the cause. As I reflect on the relationships I have built along the way, I am filled with gratitude for those who have stood by me, providing encouragement and inspiration during the most challenging times.

As we look to the future of LGBTQ rights, it is essential to harness this sense of gratitude as a catalyst for change. By recognizing the opportunities we have to make a difference, we can inspire others to join the movement. The act of expressing gratitude can also serve as a rallying cry, encouraging individuals to take action in their own communities. Whether through education, advocacy, or simply standing in solidarity, every effort counts.

In conclusion, my journey as an LGBTQ activist has been marked by profound moments of gratitude. Each opportunity to advocate for change has reinforced my commitment to the cause and highlighted the interconnectedness of our struggles. As we continue to fight for equality, let us carry this gratitude forward, transforming it into a powerful force for good. Together, we can create a world where everyone, regardless of their sexual orientation or gender identity, can live freely and authentically. Let us embrace the opportunities before us and inspire others to do the same, for in gratitude lies the power to make a lasting difference.

Encouraging readers to take action for LGBTQ rights

In a world where the battle for LGBTQ rights continues to unfold, each one of us holds the power to make a difference. The journey toward equality is not just a fight for a marginalized group; it is a fight for humanity, dignity, and the recognition of love in all its forms. As we reflect on the strides made and the challenges that remain, it is crucial to understand how individual actions can contribute to a broader movement for change.

Understanding the Importance of Advocacy

Advocacy is not merely a profession; it is a responsibility that each of us shares. According to the *Social Change Model of Leadership Development*, effective leadership is rooted in a commitment to social justice and the empowerment of others. This model emphasizes the importance of collaboration, which is essential in the fight for LGBTQ rights. When we come together as allies, we amplify our voices and enhance our impact.

$$\text{Impact} = \text{Collaboration} \times \text{Awareness} \tag{29}$$

This equation illustrates that the impact of our advocacy efforts increases exponentially when we work together and raise awareness about LGBTQ issues. Therefore, it is imperative that we educate ourselves and others about the challenges faced by the LGBTQ community, including discrimination, violence, and the lack of legal protections.

Identifying Key Issues

To take meaningful action, we must first identify the pressing issues that require our attention. Some of these include:

- **Discrimination in Employment and Housing:** Many LGBTQ individuals face discrimination in hiring and housing, leading to economic instability. The *Equality Act* aims to provide comprehensive protections against discrimination based on sexual orientation and gender identity.

- **Transgender Rights:** Transgender individuals often encounter significant barriers to healthcare, legal recognition, and personal safety. Advocacy for policies that support transgender rights is critical for ensuring their dignity and safety.

- **Global LGBTQ Rights:** In many countries, LGBTQ individuals still face criminalization and violence. Supporting international campaigns and organizations that work to protect LGBTQ rights globally is essential for fostering change.

Taking Action

The question remains: how can we take action? Here are several practical steps that individuals can take to advocate for LGBTQ rights:

1. **Educate Yourself and Others:** Knowledge is power. Read books, watch documentaries, and engage in discussions about LGBTQ issues. Share your knowledge with friends, family, and colleagues to raise awareness.

2. **Support LGBTQ Organizations:** Contribute your time or resources to local and national LGBTQ organizations. Whether through volunteering, donating, or attending events, your support can help these organizations amplify their impact.

3. **Engage in Policy Advocacy:** Write to your elected officials, urging them to support LGBTQ-friendly legislation. Participate in rallies and advocacy campaigns to demonstrate your commitment to equality.

4. **Create Inclusive Spaces:** Whether at work, school, or in your community, strive to create inclusive environments where LGBTQ individuals feel safe and valued. This can involve implementing anti-discrimination policies and promoting diversity initiatives.

5. **Be an Ally:** Stand up against discrimination and prejudice when you witness it. Use your voice to advocate for those who may not have the same privilege or platform.

The Ripple Effect of Activism

Each action, no matter how small, contributes to a larger movement. The *Diffusion of Innovations Theory* posits that new ideas and practices spread through social systems over time. When individuals take action, they inspire others to do the same, creating a ripple effect that can lead to widespread change.

$$\text{Change} = \text{Individual Action} \times \text{Social Influence} \tag{30}$$

This equation emphasizes that individual actions, when combined with social influence, can lead to significant societal change. By encouraging others to join the fight for LGBTQ rights, we create a powerful network of advocates dedicated to promoting equality.

Conclusion

In conclusion, the fight for LGBTQ rights is far from over, and your involvement is crucial. By educating yourself, supporting advocacy efforts, and standing up for equality, you can contribute to a future where everyone, regardless of their sexual orientation or gender identity, can live freely and authentically. Remember, every action counts, and together, we can create a world that embraces love, diversity, and acceptance.

Let us rise to the occasion and be the change we wish to see. The legacy of activism is built on the shoulders of those who dare to act. Are you ready to join the movement?

Index

Milton Keynes UK
Ingram Content Group UK Ltd.
UKHW020319021124
450424UK00013B/1336

9 781779 696021